Stress Less Live More - The Art of Effective Stress Management

Atul Waghmare

Published by Atul Waghmare, 2023.

Stress – What is it?

Stress is a natural physiological and psychological response that occurs when an individual perceives a demand, challenge, or threat that exceeds their ability to cope with it. It's the body's way of preparing to deal with a difficult situation or pressure. Stress can be triggered by both positive and negative events, and it can vary in intensity and duration.

When a person experiences stress, their body goes through a series of responses known as the "fight or flight" response. This response is designed to prepare the body to react quickly to a perceived threat. Physiologically, stress can lead to changes such as increased heart rate, heightened alertness, increased blood pressure, and the release of stress hormones like cortisol and adrenaline.

There are two main types of stress:

- **Acute Stress:** This is short-term stress that occurs in response to immediate situations or events. It's the body's immediate reaction to a new challenge, danger, or demand.
- **Chronic Stress:** This is long-term stress that persists over an extended period. It can result from ongoing challenges, difficulties, or situations that cause a person to feel overwhelmed and unable to cope effectively.

While stress is a normal and adaptive response that can help us handle challenges, chronic or excessive stress can have negative effects on both physical and mental health. Prolonged stress has been linked to a range of health issues, including anxiety, depression, heart problems, digestive issues, weakened immune system, and more.

It's important to manage stress effectively to maintain overall well-being. Strategies for managing stress include practicing relaxation techniques (such as deep breathing, meditation, and yoga), maintaining a healthy lifestyle (including regular exercise and a balanced diet), setting realistic goals, seeking social support, and learning effective time management and problem-solving skills.

If you find that stress is significantly impacting your daily life or well-being, consider seeking support from friends, family, or a mental health professional who can provide guidance and coping strategies.

How stress gets build up?

S tress can build up gradually over time or arise suddenly in response to specific situations. It's important to understand that stress is a complex interaction between external stressors (situations or events) and internal factors (your perception and response to those stressors). Here's how stress can build up:

- **Stressors:** Stressors are external factors or situations that trigger the stress response. They can be related to work, relationships, financial issues, health concerns, life changes, and more. Stressors can vary widely and are unique to each individual.
- **Perception:** How you perceive and interpret a stressor plays a crucial role in determining your stress level. A situation that is stressful for one person might not be stressful for another, depending on individual experiences, beliefs, and coping mechanisms.
- **Accumulation:** Everyday challenges and minor stressors can accumulate over time. These might include deadlines, traffic, household responsibilities, and other daily hassles. While individually they might not seem overwhelming, their cumulative impact can contribute to overall stress.
- **Major Life Events:** Significant life events such as moving, job changes, marriage, divorce, loss of a loved one, or health issues can create significant stress. These events can disrupt routines and require coping with new situations.

- **Lack of Coping Strategies:** If you lack effective coping strategies or resilience skills, even small stressors can build up because you might struggle to manage them well.
- **Chronic Stressors:** Long-term stressors like ongoing work pressure, relationship difficulties, financial strain, or health problems can lead to chronic stress. This type of stress can accumulate gradually and have lasting effects on your well-being.
- **Internal Factors:** Factors such as personality traits, genetic predispositions, and underlying mental health conditions can influence how you respond to stressors. Some individuals may naturally have a lower threshold for stress, making them more susceptible to feeling overwhelmed.
- **Lack of Self-Care:** Neglecting self-care, such as proper sleep, regular exercise, a balanced diet, and relaxation, can weaken your ability to handle stress. This can lead to stress building up over time.
- **Unresolved Issues:** Unresolved conflicts, unaddressed emotions, or unmet needs can contribute to a background level of stress that accumulates as time goes on.

It's important to recognize the signs of building stress and to implement healthy coping strategies before it becomes overwhelming. Regular self-care, effective problem-solving skills, seeking support from friends and family, and practicing relaxation techniques can all help prevent the buildup of excessive stress. If you find that stress is impacting your daily functioning and well-being, consider seeking professional help from a therapist or counsellor.

Stressors

S tressors are the external factors or events that trigger the stress response in individuals. When you encounter stressors, your body and mind react in various ways to prepare you to deal with the perceived challenges or threats. Here's how stress from stressors works:

- **Perception and Appraisal:** When you encounter a stressor, your brain evaluates the situation to determine whether it's a threat or a challenge. This appraisal process involves assessing the potential impact of the stressor on your well-being and resources.
- **Fight or Flight Response:** If the stressor is perceived as a threat, your body activates the "fight or flight" response. This involves releasing stress hormones like cortisol and adrenaline. These hormones prepare your body to either confront the threat (fight) or flee from it (flight).
- **Physiological Changes:** The release of stress hormones triggers various physiological changes. Your heart rate increases, your breathing becomes rapid, your muscles tense up, and your senses become heightened. These changes are meant to provide you with the energy and focus needed to respond to the stressor.
- **Attention and Focus:** In response to stressors, your attention becomes more focused on the source of stress. This narrowing of focus can help you address the stressor, but it might also lead to tunnel vision and a reduced ability to see the bigger

picture.

- **Emotional Responses:** Stressors can evoke a range of emotions, including anxiety, frustration, anger, and fear. These emotional responses are part of the body's natural way of preparing for action in the face of a perceived challenge.
- **Cognitive Changes:** Stressors can affect your cognitive functioning. You might find it difficult to concentrate, make decisions, or think clearly when under stress. This is because the body's resources are directed toward dealing with the immediate stressor.
- **Behavioural Responses:** Stressors can influence your behaviour. You might become more alert and cautious, take action to address the stressor, or even avoid situations that you associate with stress.
- **Short-Term vs. Long-Term Effects:** Acute stress responses to immediate stressors are generally temporary and subside once the stressor is dealt with or removed. However, if stressors persist or if you're exposed to multiple stressors over time, chronic stress can develop, leading to a range of physical and mental health issues.

It's important to recognize and manage stress from stressors effectively. Coping strategies can include relaxation techniques, mindfulness, exercise, seeking social support, problem-solving, time management, and seeking professional help if stress becomes overwhelming or chronic. Managing stress involves finding healthy ways to respond to stressors, building resilience, and maintaining your overall well-being.

Perceptions Stress

Stress from perceptions refers to the stress that arises from how you interpret and appraise situations, events, or circumstances in your life. It's not just the external events themselves that lead to stress, but rather your subjective understanding and evaluation of those events. This process is closely tied to cognitive appraisal, where you assess the significance of a situation and its potential impact on your well-being. Here's how stress from perceptions works:

- **Subjective Interpretation:** When you encounter a situation, your mind interprets and evaluates it based on your beliefs, values, past experiences, and personal expectations. This interpretation is subjective and can vary from person to person.

- **Positive vs. Negative Appraisal:** Your appraisal of a situation can be either positive or negative. If you perceive a situation as positive or manageable, it's likely to cause less stress. Conversely, if you view a situation as threatening, overwhelming, or beyond your coping abilities, it's more likely to lead to stress.

- **Cognitive Distortions:** Sometimes, individuals engage in cognitive distortions, which are irrational thought patterns that can contribute to negative appraisals. These distortions might include catastrophizing (assuming the worst outcome), black-and-white thinking (seeing things in extreme terms), or overgeneralization (applying a negative event to all situations).

- **Amplification:** Your perception of stressors can amplify their impact. For example, if you believe that a minor setback is a catastrophe, your stress response may be heightened, even though the situation objectively might not warrant such a strong reaction.
- **Rumination:** Dwelling on negative perceptions and thoughts, known as rumination, can intensify stress. Continuously replaying negative scenarios in your mind can prolong the stress response.
- **Self-Efficacy:** Your belief in your ability to cope with and manage situations affects your stress levels. Higher levels of self-efficacy can reduce stress because you believe you have the resources to handle challenges.
- **Control and Predictability:** A lack of control or predictability in a situation can contribute to stress. Feeling that you have no influence over the outcome can lead to increased feelings of helplessness and stress.
- **Mindfulness and Perspective:** Mindfulness, the practice of being present in the moment without judgment, can help you observe your perceptions objectively and reduce their influence on your stress response. Gaining perspective and challenging negative interpretations can also mitigate stress.

Managing stress from perceptions involves cultivating awareness of your thought patterns, challenging negative thinking, practicing cognitive reframing, and developing skills to appraise situations more realistically. By addressing the way, you perceive and interpret events, you can influence your stress response and overall well-being.

Accumulations

Stress from accumulation, often referred to as "cumulative stress" or "stress overload," occurs when multiple stressors or demands accumulate over time, leading to a sustained and overwhelming stress response. This type of stress can result from an accumulation of various factors, situations, or responsibilities that individually might not be extremely stressful but collectively contribute to a significant burden on your physical and mental well-being. Here's how stress from accumulation works:

- **Multiple Stressors:** Accumulated stress can stem from various sources such as work, family, relationships, financial pressures, health concerns, and personal responsibilities. Each stressor on its own might be manageable, but their combined effect can be overwhelming.

- **Limited Recovery Time:** When stressors are constant or overlapping, you might have limited time to recover and recharge between them. This can prevent your body and mind from fully recuperating from the stress response.

- **Amplification:** Each new stressor can amplify the impact of existing stressors. Stressors can feed off each other, intensifying your overall stress response.

- **Limited Coping Resources:** Coping with stress requires physical, emotional, and cognitive resources. Accumulated stress can deplete these resources, making it more challenging to effectively manage additional stressors.

- **Chronic Stress:** When stressors accumulate without sufficient relief, chronic stress can develop. Chronic stress is linked to various physical and mental health issues, including anxiety, depression, cardiovascular problems, and more.
- **Decreased Resilience:** Prolonged exposure to stressors can decrease your resilience, making it harder to cope with new challenges as they arise.
- **Impact on Decision-Making:** Accumulated stress can cloud your judgment and decision-making abilities. It becomes difficult to assess situations objectively and make well-informed choices.
- **Physical Health Impact:** Chronic stress can lead to physiological changes, such as increased blood pressure, compromised immune function, and digestive issues, all of which can further contribute to overall health problems.

Managing stress from accumulation involves several strategies:

- **Prioritization:** Assess your responsibilities and commitments, and prioritize tasks based on urgency and importance.
- **Time Management:** Effective time management can help you allocate time to various tasks and responsibilities, reducing the feeling of being overwhelmed.
- **Boundary Setting:** Set boundaries to protect your time and well-being. Learn to say no to additional responsibilities when necessary.
- **Self-Care:** Regular self-care practices, such as exercise, relaxation techniques, and hobbies, can help you recharge and build resilience against accumulated stress.
- **Support System:** Seek support from friends, family, or professionals to share your feelings and challenges, and gain

insights into managing stress.

- **Problem-Solving:** Develop effective problem-solving skills to tackle challenges and find solutions for stressors.
- **Mindfulness:** Practicing mindfulness can help you stay present and manage stressors as they arise, without becoming overwhelmed by their accumulation.

Recognizing the signs of accumulated stress and implementing strategies to address it can help prevent burnout and promote overall well-being. If stress becomes overwhelming, consider seeking support from a mental health professional.

Major life events

Stress from major life events refers to the stress that arises from significant changes or transitions in life that have a profound impact on your routine, emotions, and overall well-being. These events can be positive or negative, but they often involve a degree of disruption and adjustment. Major life events can trigger strong emotional and physiological responses due to the challenges they present. Here's how stress from major life events works:

- **Transition and Change:** Major life events represent significant shifts from your usual circumstances. These transitions can involve changes in roles, relationships, routines, and responsibilities.
- **Positive and Negative Events:** Major life events can encompass a wide range of experiences, from positive events like marriage, childbirth, or promotions, to negative events such as divorce, loss of a loved one, or job loss.
- **Emotional Impact:** Major life events often evoke strong emotions, including joy, grief, excitement, anxiety, and sadness. These emotions can contribute to stress as you navigate the complexities of your feelings.
- **Disruption of Routine:** Major life events can disrupt your daily routine and force you to adapt to new circumstances. The uncertainty and unfamiliarity of these changes can trigger stress.
- **Coping with Change:** Adjusting to major life events requires

coping skills and resilience to effectively manage the associated stressors.

- **Support Systems:** Social support from friends, family, and professionals can play a crucial role in helping you navigate major life events and alleviate stress.
- **Cognitive Processing:** Major life events might require you to process new information, make important decisions, and reevaluate your goals. These cognitive demands can contribute to stress.
- **Physical Responses:** Stress from major life events can lead to physiological changes, including increased heart rate, elevated blood pressure, and changes in sleep patterns.

Common major life events that can trigger stress include:

- Marriage or divorce
- Birth or adoption of a child
- Death of a loved one
- Relocation or moving to a new place
- Starting or ending a significant relationship
- Career changes, such as job loss or retirement
- Serious illness or injury
- Financial challenges
- Educational milestones

Managing stress from major life events involves a combination of strategies:

- **Self-Care:** Prioritize self-care activities that promote relaxation, exercise, healthy eating, and sufficient sleep.
- **Seeking Support:** Reach out to friends, family, or professionals to share your feelings and gain insights into managing the stress associated with major life events.

- **Mindfulness:** Practicing mindfulness can help you stay grounded in the present moment and manage the emotions that arise from major life changes.
- **Effective Communication:** Communicate your needs and emotions to those around you, helping them understand your perspective and provide support.
- **Problem-Solving:** Develop problem-solving skills to address challenges that arise from major life events and make informed decisions.
- **Seeking Professional Help:** If you find that the stress from major life events is overwhelming or affecting your well-being, consider seeking support from a therapist or counsellor.

Recognizing the impact of major life events on your stress levels and implementing effective coping strategies can help you navigate these transitions with resilience and well-being.

Lack of Coping Strategies

Stress from a lack of coping strategies refers to the heightened stress response that occurs when you encounter challenges or stressors without having effective ways to manage or deal with them. Coping strategies are essential tools that help you navigate difficulties and reduce the negative impact of stress on your physical and mental well-being. When you lack these strategies, stress can become overwhelming and have a more significant impact on your life. Here's how stress from a lack of coping strategies works:

- **Unmanaged Stressors:** Stressors are a part of life, but without coping strategies, you may find it difficult to manage their effects. This can lead to increased stress levels and difficulties in handling various situations.
- **Emotional Overload:** When you lack coping strategies, emotions related to stressors can become overwhelming. You might feel anxious, frustrated, or even helpless in the face of challenges.
- **Physical Response:** The absence of coping strategies can lead to intensified physiological responses to stress, including increased heart rate, muscle tension, and changes in breathing patterns.
- **Negative Coping:** Without healthy coping strategies, you might resort to negative coping mechanisms such as excessive alcohol or substance use, emotional eating, or avoidance, which can exacerbate stress and create new problems.

- **Cycle of Stress:** A lack of coping strategies can lead to a cycle of stress, where the inability to manage stressors increases stress levels, which in turn makes it even harder to cope.
- **Rumination:** Without effective strategies to manage thoughts and emotions, rumination (dwelling on negative thoughts) can become more common, intensifying the impact of stressors.
- **Impact on Mental Health:** Prolonged stress without coping strategies can contribute to the development or exacerbation of mental health issues such as anxiety and depression.
- **Interpersonal Relationships:** Stress without healthy coping strategies can strain relationships with friends, family, and colleagues due to emotional distress and impaired communication.

To address stress from a lack of coping strategies:

- **Learn Coping Techniques:** Educate yourself about healthy coping mechanisms such as deep breathing, meditation, mindfulness, and progressive muscle relaxation.
- **Practice Self-Care:** Engage in self-care activities that promote relaxation, physical health, and emotional well-being.
- **Develop Problem-Solving Skills:** Learn problem-solving techniques to address challenges and find solutions rather than becoming overwhelmed.
- **Seek Support:** Reach out to friends, family, or professionals who can provide guidance, support, and perspectives on managing stress.
- **Build Resilience:** Focus on building resilience, which enables you to adapt to stressors more effectively and recover more quickly from challenges.

- **Professional Help:** If stress becomes overwhelming, consider seeking support from a mental health professional who can help you develop coping strategies tailored to your needs.

Remember that coping strategies are learned skills, and it's never too late to develop and enhance them. By cultivating healthy ways to manage stress, you can significantly reduce its negative impact on your life and well-being.

Chronic Stressors

Stress from chronic stressors refers to the ongoing and prolonged stress that results from continuous exposure to challenging situations, demands, or conditions. Unlike acute stressors, which are short-term and immediate, chronic stressors persist over an extended period, leading to a sustained stress response. Chronic stressors can have significant effects on physical, emotional, and mental well-being. Here's how stress from chronic stressors works:

- **Long-Term Exposure:** Chronic stressors are persistent and recurrent challenges that you face over an extended period. These stressors can range from work-related pressures to ongoing relationship difficulties or financial strain.
- **Stress Response:** When exposed to chronic stressors, your body's stress response system remains activated over time. This can lead to continuous release of stress hormones like cortisol, resulting in physiological changes.
- **Physiological Impact:** Chronic stressors can affect various body systems, including cardiovascular, immune, and digestive systems. Over time, these effects can contribute to health issues such as hypertension, weakened immune function, and gastrointestinal problems.
- **Emotional Toll:** Dealing with chronic stressors can lead to emotional exhaustion, irritability, anxiety, and a decreased ability to manage your emotions effectively.
- **Cognitive Challenges:** Chronic stressors can impair

cognitive function, affecting memory, attention, decision-making, and problem-solving abilities.

- **Sleep Disturbances:** Chronic stressors can lead to sleep difficulties, including insomnia or disrupted sleep patterns, which in turn can further contribute to stress and fatigue.
- **Chronic Health Conditions:** Prolonged exposure to chronic stressors is associated with an increased risk of developing chronic health conditions such as cardiovascular disease, diabetes, and mental health disorders.
- **Reduced Coping Capacity:** The ongoing nature of chronic stressors can deplete your coping resources, making it harder to manage stress effectively over time.

Managing stress from chronic stressors

- **Stress Reduction Techniques:** Regularly practice stress reduction techniques such as mindfulness, deep breathing, meditation, and progressive muscle relaxation.
- **Healthy Lifestyle:** Prioritize a healthy lifestyle that includes regular exercise, balanced nutrition, sufficient sleep, and avoiding unhealthy coping mechanisms.
- **Time Management:** Develop effective time management skills to better allocate time to tasks and responsibilities, reducing the feeling of being overwhelmed.
- **Social Support:** Seek support from friends, family, or support groups to share your feelings and gain insights into managing chronic stressors.
- **Professional Help:** If chronic stressors are significantly impacting your well-being, consider seeking support from a mental health professional who can provide guidance and coping strategies.

It's essential to recognize the signs of chronic stress and take proactive steps to manage it. By addressing chronic stressors and implementing effective coping strategies, you can reduce the negative impact on your physical and mental health and improve your overall quality of life.

Internal Factors

Stress from internal factors refers to stress that originates from within yourself, such as your thoughts, beliefs, attitudes, and emotions. These internal factors can influence how you perceive and react to external situations, leading to stress responses. Internal factors play a significant role in shaping your overall stress levels and how you cope with challenges. Here's how stress from internal factors works:

- **Thought Patterns:** Negative thought patterns, such as catastrophizing (assuming the worst outcome), overgeneralization (applying a negative event to all situations), and black-and-white thinking (seeing things in extremes), can contribute to stress by amplifying perceived threats.

- **Self-Criticism:** Being overly self-critical or having low self-esteem can lead to stress as you constantly feel pressured to meet high expectations or fear making mistakes.

- **Perfectionism:** Striving for perfection and setting unrealistic standards can lead to chronic stress as you place constant pressure on yourself to achieve flawlessness.

- **Negative Self-Talk:** Engaging in negative self-talk, where you consistently criticize or doubt yourself, can contribute to feelings of stress and inadequacy.

- **Emotional Regulation:** Difficulty regulating emotions, such as excessive worry, anger, or fear, can increase stress responses to various situations.

- **Mindset:** A fixed mindset, where you believe that your abilities and qualities are innate and unchangeable, can lead to stress when faced with challenges that you perceive as threatening to your self-image.
- **Uncertainty:** An inability to tolerate uncertainty or ambiguity can lead to heightened stress in situations where outcomes are unclear.
- **Control Issues:** A strong need for control over situations can lead to stress when faced with circumstances that are beyond your control.
- **Negative Beliefs:** Deep-seated negative beliefs about yourself, the world, or the future can lead to a pessimistic outlook, contributing to stress.
- **Rumination:** Repeatedly dwelling on negative thoughts or events, known as rumination, can intensify stress by perpetuating negative emotions.

Managing stress from internal factors

- **Cognitive Restructuring:** Challenge and reframe negative thought patterns to promote more balanced and realistic thinking.
- **Self-Compassion:** Practice self-compassion by treating yourself with kindness and understanding, reducing self-criticism.
- **Mindfulness:** Cultivate mindfulness to become aware of your thoughts and emotions in the present moment without judgment, helping you respond to stress more skilfully.
- **Emotion Regulation:** Develop skills to regulate your emotions, allowing you to manage intense feelings and respond more calmly to stressors.
- **Positive Self-Talk:** Replace negative self-talk with positive and affirming statements to boost your self-esteem and resilience.
- **Growth Mindset:** Cultivate a growth mindset, where you believe that challenges are opportunities for growth and improvement.
- **Seeking Support:** If internal factors are significantly affecting your well-being, consider seeking support from a therapist or counsellor who can help you address and manage these factors.

Recognizing the influence of internal factors on your stress levels and actively working to shift negative patterns can lead to improved stress management and overall well-being.

Lack of Self-Care

Stress from a lack of self-care refers to the increased stress that arises when you neglect to prioritize your own well-being, health, and mental and emotional needs. Self-care involves engaging in activities and practices that nourish and rejuvenate you, helping to reduce the negative impact of stress and maintain overall balance. When self-care is lacking, stress can accumulate and take a toll on various aspects of your life. Here's how stress from a lack of self-care works:

- **Neglected Physical Health:** When you neglect proper nutrition, exercise, and sleep, your body can become more vulnerable to stress and less equipped to handle its effects.
- **Emotional Exhaustion:** A lack of self-care can lead to emotional exhaustion, making it challenging to manage stressors and regulate your emotions effectively.
- **Reduced Resilience:** Without self-care, your ability to bounce back from stressors and challenges may decrease, making you more susceptible to feeling overwhelmed.
- **Diminished Coping Resources:** Engaging in self-care activities replenishes your coping resources, but without them, your capacity to manage stress is compromised.
- **Physical Symptoms:** Neglecting self-care can lead to physical symptoms such as headaches, muscle tension, fatigue, and digestive problems, which can amplify stress.
- **Mental Health Impact:** A lack of self-care can exacerbate or contribute to mental health issues such as anxiety and

depression.

- **Quality of Life:** Without regular self-care, your overall quality of life can decline as stress takes a toll on your physical, emotional, and social well-being.
- **Impaired Relationships:** Stress from a lack of self-care can spill over into your relationships, affecting your interactions with family, friends, and colleagues.

To address stress from a lack of self-care:

- **Prioritize Well-Being:** Recognize the importance of self-care and make it a priority in your daily routine.
- **Regular Exercise:** Engage in regular physical activity that supports your physical and mental health.
- **Healthy Nutrition:** Maintain a balanced diet that provides essential nutrients for optimal functioning.
- **Adequate Sleep:** Ensure you're getting sufficient sleep to support your body's recovery and resilience.
- **Mindfulness and Relaxation:** Practice mindfulness, deep breathing, meditation, and relaxation techniques to manage stress.
- **Hobbies and Activities:** Engage in activities you enjoy that bring you joy and help you unwind.
- **Boundaries:** Set boundaries to ensure you're not overextending yourself and neglecting your needs.
- **Seeking Support:** If you struggle with prioritizing self-care, seek support from friends, family, or professionals who can help you establish healthy habits.

Recognizing the importance of self-care and taking intentional steps to incorporate it into your daily life can help you manage stress more effectively and improve your overall well-being.

Unresolved Issues

Stress from unresolved issues refers to the stress that arises when you have ongoing, unresolved problems, conflicts, or concerns that you haven't addressed or managed effectively. These unresolved issues can linger in the background, contributing to a persistent state of stress and unease. They can have a significant impact on your mental, emotional, and physical well-being. Here's how stress from unresolved issues works:

- **Persistent Preoccupation:** Unresolved issues can occupy your thoughts and attention, making it difficult to focus on other tasks and leading to increased stress.
- **Emotional Burden:** Lingering unresolved issues can lead to emotional distress, anxiety, and a sense of unease as you grapple with unresolved emotions.
- **Impact on Relationships:** Unresolved issues can strain relationships with family, friends, or colleagues, leading to conflicts and misunderstandings that contribute to stress.
- **Delayed Problem-Solving:** Avoiding or neglecting to address problems can delay their resolution, prolonging the stress associated with those issues.
- **Negative Coping Mechanisms:** In an attempt to manage the stress from unresolved issues, individuals might resort to negative coping mechanisms such as avoidance, denial, or unhealthy behaviours.
- **Rumination:** Unresolved issues can lead to rumination,

where you continuously replay and analyse the issue in your mind, intensifying the stress response.

- **Physical Symptoms:** The chronic stress from unresolved issues can manifest as physical symptoms such as tension, headaches, sleep disturbances, and digestive problems.
- **Impact on Self-Esteem:** Unresolved issues can affect your self-esteem and self-worth, contributing to stress and feelings of inadequacy.

To address stress from unresolved issues:

- **Identify the Issues:** Acknowledge the specific issues or concerns that are causing stress and recognize their impact on your well-being.
- **Effective Communication:** If the issues involve other people, practice effective communication to address concerns, clarify misunderstandings, and seek resolution.
- **Problem-Solving:** Develop problem-solving skills to approach the issues systematically and find viable solutions.
- **Seek Professional Help:** If the issues are complex or emotionally challenging, consider seeking support from a therapist or counsellor who can provide guidance and strategies.
- **Closure and Acceptance:** Sometimes, resolution might involve accepting things you cannot change and finding ways to move forward positively.
- **Forgiveness:** If the issue involves a conflict with another person, consider the potential benefits of forgiveness for your own well-being.
- **Self-Compassion:** Be compassionate with yourself as you work through unresolved issues, recognizing that healing takes time.

Addressing and resolving unresolved issues can alleviate stress and contribute to improved emotional well-being. Taking steps to face challenges, communicate effectively, and find closure can lead to a greater sense of peace and balance in your life.

Stress in children

Stress in children is a common and normal response to various situations and challenges they encounter in their lives. However, excessive or chronic stress can have negative effects on their physical, emotional, and psychological well-being. Here are some key points to understand about stress in children:

- **Causes of Stress:** Children can experience stress due to a wide range of factors, including academic pressures, social interactions, family dynamics, extracurricular activities, health issues, changes in routine, and exposure to traumatic events.
- **Signs of Stress:** Children may exhibit both physical and emotional signs of stress. Physical signs can include changes in appetite, sleep disturbances, headaches, stomach-aches, and fatigue. Emotional signs may involve increased irritability, mood swings, anxiety, clinginess, withdrawal from activities, and changes in behaviour.
- **Age-Related Stressors:** Different age groups experience stress differently. Younger children might struggle with separation anxiety, while adolescents may grapple with academic pressures, social identity, and peer relationships.
- **Academic Pressure:** School-related stress can stem from the expectations to perform well academically, complete assignments, excel in exams, and balance extracurricular activities. Standardized testing can also contribute to stress.

- **Social Pressures:** Peer interactions, bullying, social acceptance, and fitting in can be sources of stress for children. Adolescents may experience additional stress related to romantic relationships, body image, and identity.
- **Family Dynamics:** Conflict within the family, changes in family structure, parental expectations, and financial difficulties can all contribute to stress in children.
- **Coping Mechanisms:** Children often lack well-developed coping skills to manage stress effectively. Some children may engage in unhealthy behaviours such as overeating, withdrawal, aggression, or substance use as coping mechanisms.
- **Supportive Environment:** Creating a supportive and open environment at home and school is crucial for helping children manage stress. Encourage open communication and provide opportunities for children to express their feelings.
- **Teaching Coping Skills:** Teaching children healthy coping strategies, such as deep breathing, mindfulness, physical activity, creative outlets, and problem-solving, can empower them to handle stress better.
- **Balancing Activities:** While extracurricular activities can be enriching, an overload of commitments can contribute to stress. It's important to find a balance that allows time for relaxation and free play.
- **Modelling Behaviour:** Parents and caregivers play a significant role in modelling healthy stress management techniques. Demonstrating effective coping strategies sets a positive example for children to follow.
- **Seeking Professional Help:** If a child's stress is interfering with their daily functioning or seems to be escalating, seeking help from a mental health professional, such as a child psychologist or counsellor, can provide valuable support.

Remember that stress is a normal part of life, and helping children learn to manage it is an important life skill. By providing them with the tools and support they need, you can help them navigate stressful situations more effectively and build resilience for the future.

Stress in women

Stress in women is a significant and complex issue that can be influenced by a variety of biological, psychological, social, and cultural factors. Women often experience unique stressors and challenges that can impact their physical and mental well-being. Here are some key considerations when it comes to stress in women:

Biological Factors:

Hormonal Changes: Women experience hormonal fluctuations throughout their menstrual cycle, pregnancy, and menopause. These hormonal changes can influence mood and stress levels.

Postpartum Period: Postpartum depression and anxiety can contribute to high stress levels in new mothers.

Chronic Health Conditions: Women may be more susceptible to certain health conditions, such as autoimmune disorders or thyroid issues, which can exacerbate stress.

Psychological Factors:

Multiple Roles: Many women juggle various roles, such as being a caregiver, parent, employee, and partner. Balancing these roles can lead to feelings of overwhelm.

Perfectionism: Societal and self-imposed expectations for women to excel in multiple areas of life can create perfectionism, leading to increased stress.

Body Image and Self-Esteem: Societal pressures related to body image can contribute to stress and low self-esteem.

Social and Cultural Factors:

Gender Inequality: Women may face gender-based discrimination, unequal pay, and limited opportunities, which can contribute to chronic stress.

Caregiving Responsibilities: Women often take on a larger share of caregiving responsibilities for children, elderly family members, and other dependents.

Social Support: Strong social connections and support networks can help mitigate stress, but women may also face barriers to seeking support due to societal norms.

Life Transitions:

Motherhood: While motherhood can be rewarding, it also comes with significant demands and adjustments that can lead to increased stress.

Menopause: Hormonal changes during menopause can contribute to mood swings, anxiety, and stress.

Mental Health:

Women are more likely than men to experience conditions like depression and anxiety, which can heighten stress levels.

Workplace Stress:

Balancing Work and Family: The pressure to manage both career and family responsibilities can be a major source of stress for women.

Discrimination and Harassment: Women may face workplace discrimination, harassment, and unequal treatment, leading to chronic stress.

Coping Strategies:

Women tend to seek social support and engage in "tend-and-befriend" responses, where they nurture social connections to cope with stress.

Engaging in relaxation techniques, physical activity, mindfulness, and creative outlets can be effective coping strategies.

Self-Care:

Prioritizing self-care is crucial for managing stress. This can include setting boundaries, engaging in activities that bring joy, and taking time for oneself.

Professional Help:

If stress becomes overwhelming or chronic, seeking support from mental health professionals, such as therapists or counsellors, can provide valuable assistance.

Recognizing the unique stressors women face and fostering an environment that supports their well-being is essential. Encouraging open conversations about stress, promoting work-life balance, advocating for gender equality, and providing access to resources can help women better manage stress and improve their overall quality of life.

Hormonal changes can significantly impact stress levels in women due to the intricate relationship between hormones and mood regulation. Throughout a woman's life, various stages and events can trigger hormonal fluctuations that contribute to stress. Here are some key hormonal changes and their potential impact on stress in women:

- **Menstrual Cycle:**
  - Premenstrual Syndrome (PMS): Many women experience mood changes, irritability, and heightened stress during the days leading up to their menstrual period. This is often referred to as premenstrual syndrome (PMS).
  - Premenstrual Dysphoric Disorder (PMDD): In some cases, the symptoms of PMS can be severe and significantly impact daily functioning. This is known

as premenstrual dysphoric disorder (PMDD), which includes symptoms such as extreme mood swings, anxiety, and depression.

- **Pregnancy:**
  - Hormonal changes during pregnancy, particularly elevated levels of oestrogen and progesterone, can lead to mood swings, anxiety, and stress.
  - Stress during pregnancy is concerning, as excessive stress may impact fatal development and increase the risk of complications.

- **Postpartum Period:**
  - After giving birth, the abrupt drop in hormone levels can contribute to the development of postpartum mood disorders, such as postpartum depression and anxiety. These disorders can cause significant stress for new mothers.

- **Perimenopause and Menopause:**
  - Perimenopause, the transitional phase leading to menopause, is marked by hormonal fluctuations. These changes can contribute to mood swings, irritability, and increased stress.
  - Menopause, characterized by the cessation of menstruation, involves significant hormonal shifts. These changes can affect mood regulation and increase the risk of mood disorders.

- **Oral Contraceptives and Hormone Therapy:**
  - Some women may experience mood changes and stress-related symptoms as a result of using oral contraceptives or hormone replacement therapy.

- **Stress-Hormone Relationship:**
  - Stress itself can influence hormone levels. Chronic stress can lead to an overproduction of cortisol, the

body's primary stress hormone. Elevated cortisol levels can disrupt hormonal balance and contribute to mood disturbances.

- **Coping Strategies:**
  - Recognizing the connection between hormonal changes and stress can empower women to implement effective coping strategies.
  - Engaging in regular exercise, practicing relaxation techniques (e.g., deep breathing, meditation), maintaining a balanced diet, and getting adequate sleep can help mitigate stress.
- **Professional Support:**
  - If hormonal changes are causing significant distress and interfering with daily functioning, seeking support from mental health professionals, gynaecologists, or endocrinologists is recommended.

It's important for women to be aware of the potential impact of hormonal changes on their stress levels and mental well-being. Developing a proactive approach to managing stress, building a strong support network, and seeking professional help when needed can help women navigate hormonal fluctuations and maintain their overall health and happiness.

Stress in Old age

Stress in old age, also known as late-life or geriatric stress, can stem from a variety of factors associated with the challenges and changes that come with aging. While stress is a normal response to life's demands, excessive or chronic stress in older adults can have significant physical, emotional, and cognitive impacts. Here are some key considerations regarding stress in old age:

- **Health Challenges:**
    - Age-related health issues such as chronic illnesses, mobility limitations, pain, and cognitive decline can contribute to stress.
    - Managing multiple medications, doctor visits, and health-related decisions can be overwhelming.

- **Loss and Grief:**
    - Older adults may experience the loss of loved ones, friends, or peers more frequently, leading to grief and feelings of isolation.
    - Retirement, loss of identity tied to work, and changes in social circles can also contribute to feelings of loss and stress.

- **Financial Concerns:**
    - Limited income, medical expenses, and concerns about long-term care and financial security can lead to stress.
    - Social security, pension, and retirement savings may

not be sufficient to cover expenses.

- **Social Isolation:**
    - ○ Reduced mobility, loss of driving privileges, and the passing of friends can lead to social isolation, increasing the risk of stress and depression.
- **Family Dynamics:**
    - ○ Aging adults may experience role reversals as they become dependent on their adult children or caregivers. This change can lead to feelings of loss of control and stress.
- **Cognitive Changes:**
    - ○ Cognitive decline and memory impairment can lead to frustration and stress, especially when performing daily tasks or making decisions.
- **Transition to Care Facilities:**
    - ○ Moving to a nursing home, assisted living facility, or other care setting can be stressful due to the loss of independence and familiar surroundings.
- **Fear of Death:**
    - ○ The awareness of mortality and fear of death can contribute to existential stress and anxiety.
- **Coping Strategies:**
    - ○ Engaging in hobbies, physical activities, and social interactions can help reduce stress and improve overall well-being.
    - ○ Participating in support groups and maintaining close relationships with friends and family members can provide emotional support.
- **Mindfulness and Relaxation:**
    - ○ Practices such as mindfulness, meditation, deep breathing, and yoga can help manage stress and promote relaxation.

- **Professional Help:**
  - If stress becomes overwhelming and starts affecting daily functioning, seeking support from mental health professionals, such as therapists or counsellors, can be beneficial.
- **Healthy Lifestyle:**
  - A balanced diet, regular exercise, adequate sleep, and staying hydrated can contribute to better stress management and overall health.

Understanding the unique stressors that older adults face and creating a supportive environment that addresses their needs is crucial. Open communication, maintaining social connections, and seeking appropriate support can help older adults navigate the challenges of aging while maintaining a good quality of life.

OLD AGE STRESS THAT triggers panic mode can be distressing and overwhelming for older adults. Panic attacks are intense episodes of fear and anxiety accompanied by physical symptoms. They can be particularly challenging for seniors to manage due to potential health conditions, limited coping mechanisms, and other age-related factors. Here are some steps to help manage old age stress and panic mode:

- **Recognize the Signs:**
  - Understand the symptoms of panic attacks, which may include rapid heartbeat, shortness of breath, sweating, trembling, chest pain, dizziness, and a sense of impending doom.
- **Practice Relaxation Techniques:**
  - Engage in relaxation techniques such as deep breathing, mindfulness, progressive muscle

relaxation, and meditation. These methods can help calm the body's stress response.

- **Grounding Techniques:**
  - Use grounding techniques to stay connected to the present moment. Focus on your surroundings, touch a comforting object, or practice counting to stay centred.

- **Stay in a Safe Space:**
  - If a panic attack occurs, find a safe and quiet place to sit or lie down. Remove yourself from overwhelming situations if possible.

- **Breathing Exercises:**
  - Practice slow, deep breathing to regulate your heart rate and calm your nervous system. Inhale deeply for a count of four, hold for four, exhale for four, and pause for four.

- **Mindful Distraction:**
  - Engage in an activity that requires focus, such as counting backwards, reciting a poem, or describing an object in detail. This can help divert your attention from panic symptoms.

- **Seek Support:**
  - Reach out to a friend, family member, or caregiver who can provide reassurance and assistance during a panic attack.

- **Stay Hydrated and Nourished:**
  - Dehydration and low blood sugar can contribute to feelings of anxiety and panic. Ensure you're staying hydrated and consuming balanced meals.

- **Limit Stimulants:**
  - Reduce or avoid caffeine, nicotine, and other stimulants, as they can exacerbate anxiety symptoms.

- **Stay Active:**
    - Regular physical activity can help regulate mood and reduce stress. Engage in activities that you enjoy and are appropriate for your physical abilities.
- **Consider Professional Help:**
    - If panic attacks and stress are interfering with your daily life, consider seeking support from a mental health professional who specializes in treating older adults.
- **Medication:**
    - In some cases, a doctor may prescribe medication to manage severe anxiety or panic symptoms. Consult a healthcare professional for guidance.
- **Build a Support System:**
    - Maintain connections with friends, family, and support groups. Social interaction can provide emotional support and reduce feelings of isolation.
- **Mind-Body Practices:**
    - Explore practices like Tai Chi, gentle yoga, or breathing exercises tailored for older adults. These practices can help promote relaxation and balance.

Remember that managing panic attacks and stress requires patience and practice. Developing a toolkit of coping strategies that work best for you can empower you to navigate panic mode and find a sense of calm and control.

Business stress

Business stress is a common experience for entrepreneurs, business owners, and employees working in fast-paced and competitive environments. Managing and coping with business-related stress is crucial for maintaining well-being and achieving success. Here are some strategies to help manage business stress:

- **Time Management:**
    - Prioritize tasks and create a daily schedule. Time management techniques like the Pomodoro Technique (working in focused intervals) can help increase productivity and reduce stress.
- **Set Realistic Goals:**
    - Set achievable goals that align with your resources and time. Unrealistic expectations can lead to undue stress and burnout.
- **Delegate and Outsource:**
    - Delegate tasks to team members or consider outsourcing tasks that are not within your core competencies. Sharing the workload can alleviate stress.
- **Effective Communication:**
    - Maintain clear communication with team members, clients, and stakeholders. Addressing issues promptly and transparently can prevent misunderstandings and reduce stress.

- **Work-Life Balance:**
  - Set boundaries between work and personal life. Allocate time for relaxation, hobbies, and spending time with loved ones to recharge.
- **Stress-Reduction Techniques:**
  - Engage in stress-reduction activities such as exercise, meditation, deep breathing, and mindfulness to relax the mind and body.
- **Problem-Solving Skills:**
  - Develop strong problem-solving skills to address challenges and setbacks with a constructive mindset.
- **Healthy Lifestyle:**
  - Eat a balanced diet, get regular exercise, maintain good sleep hygiene, and avoid excessive caffeine and alcohol intake. A healthy lifestyle supports better stress management.
- **Social Support:**
  - Seek support from mentors, peers, and networking groups. Sharing experiences and advice with others in similar situations can help alleviate stress.
- **Mindfulness and Self-Care:**
  - Practice mindfulness to stay present and reduce rumination about past mistakes or future worries. Prioritize self-care and engage in activities that bring you joy.
- **Learn to Say No:**
  - Avoid overcommitting. Learning to say no to additional responsibilities when your plate is already full can prevent burnout.
- **Seek Professional Help:**
  - If stress becomes overwhelming and starts affecting your mental and physical health, consider seeking

support from a therapist or counsellor.

- **Financial Management:**
    - Plan and manage your business finances effectively to minimize financial stressors.
- **Flexibility and Adaptability:**
    - Embrace change and be open to adapting your strategies based on market trends and feedback. Flexibility can help reduce stress caused by rigid expectations.
- **Celebrate Achievements:**
    - Take time to acknowledge and celebrate your accomplishments, no matter how small. Positive reinforcement can help combat feelings of stress and self-doubt.

Remember that managing business stress is an ongoing process. By implementing these strategies and tailoring them to your unique situation, you can navigate the challenges of entrepreneurship and business ownership while maintaining your well-being and success.

Unemployment stress

Unemployment stress is a common and challenging experience that can have a significant impact on an individual's mental, emotional, and financial well-being. Losing a job can led to a range of negative feelings, including anxiety, frustration, and even depression. However, there are strategies you can employ to cope with unemployment stress:

- **Acknowledge Your Feelings:**
    - It's natural to feel a range of emotions after losing a job. Allow yourself to acknowledge and process these feelings without judgment.
- **Create a Routine:**
    - Establishing a daily routine can provide structure and a sense of purpose during your job search. Include activities that promote physical and mental well-being.
- **Set Realistic Goals:**
    - Break down your job search goals into manageable steps. Celebrate small victories, such as sending out resumes or networking successfully.
- **Stay Positive:**
    - Cultivate a positive mindset by focusing on your strengths, accomplishments, and potential. Avoid negative self-talk that can contribute to stress.
- **Network and Connect:**

- Reach out to friends, family, former colleagues, and industry contacts for support, advice, and potential job leads.
- **Skill Development:**
  - Use your free time to develop new skills, enhance existing ones, or pursue certifications that could make you more marketable.
- **Volunteer or Freelance:**
  - Engaging in volunteer work or freelance projects can help keep you occupied, expand your network, and enhance your resume.
- **Maintain Physical Health:**
  - Regular exercise, a balanced diet, and adequate sleep are important for managing stress and maintaining overall well-being.
- **Mindfulness and Relaxation:**
  - Practice mindfulness, meditation, deep breathing, or yoga to reduce stress and stay grounded.
- **Financial Planning:**
  - Create a budget to manage your finances during your job search. Cut unnecessary expenses and explore ways to save money.
- **Seek Support:**
  - Don't hesitate to reach out to mental health professionals, counsellors, or support groups if you're struggling with the emotional toll of unemployment.
- **Limit Isolation:**
  - Stay connected with friends, family, and social groups to prevent feelings of isolation and loneliness.
- **Explore New Opportunities:**

- ○ Use this period as an opportunity to explore new career paths, industries, or positions that you may not have considered before.
- **Practice Patience:**
  - ○ Job searches can take time, especially in competitive markets. Be patient with yourself and the process.
- **Celebrate Small Wins:**
  - ○ Acknowledge your efforts and accomplishments, even if they aren't directly related to finding a job. Every step forward is a victory.

Remember that unemployment is a temporary situation, and with perseverance and the right strategies, you can navigate this challenging time and find new opportunities for personal and professional growth.

Navigating Financial Stress- Strategies for Resilience and Well-Being

Financial stress is a prevalent and significant issue that affects individuals across various socio-economic backgrounds. It arises from the burden of managing economic challenges such as debt, job loss, unexpected expenses, and limited resources. While financial stress can have a profound impact on mental, emotional, and physical well-being, individuals have the power to employ strategies that mitigate its negative effects and promote financial resilience.

- **Understanding Financial Stress:** Financial stress is more than just a concern about money; it's an emotional and psychological response to economic uncertainties. The fear of not being able to meet basic needs or fulfil financial obligations can trigger a range of negative emotions, including anxiety, depression, and helplessness.

- **Sources of Financial Stress:** a. **Debt:** Accumulating high-interest debt can lead to a cycle of stress as individuals grapple with repayment obligations. b. **Job Insecurity:** The fear of job loss or reduced income can create instability and intensify stress. c. **Unexpected Expenses:** Sudden medical bills, home repairs, or emergencies can disrupt financial plans and trigger stress. d. **Insufficient Savings:** Not having an emergency fund can leave individuals vulnerable to unexpected financial shocks. e. **Limited Income:** Living with a constrained budget can create challenges in meeting day-to-day expenses.

- **Impact on Well-Being:** a. **Mental Health:** Financial stress can contribute to anxiety, depression, and other mental health issues. b. **Physical Health:** Chronic stress has been linked to physical health problems like heart disease, high blood pressure, and sleep disturbances. c. **Relationships:** Financial stress can strain relationships due to disagreements over money and the emotional toll it takes on individuals.

- **Strategies for Managing Financial Stress:** a. **Financial Literacy:** Educating oneself about personal finance can empower individuals to make informed decisions and reduce stress. b. **Budgeting:** Creating a budget help allocate funds to essential expenses, savings, and debt repayment. c. **Emergency Fund:** Building an emergency fund acts as a safety net during unexpected financial crises. d. **Debt Management:** Developing a debt repayment plan and seeking advice from financial professionals can alleviate stress. e. **Positive Mindset:** Cultivating a positive attitude and focusing on one's strengths can enhance resilience and reduce stress. f. **Support Network:** Engaging with friends, family, or support groups can provide emotional and social support. g. **Seeking Professional Help:** Consulting financial advisors or therapists can offer expert guidance and emotional relief.

- **Promoting Financial Resilience:** a. **Goal Setting:** Setting achievable financial goals provides a sense of direction and purpose. b. **Adaptability:** Being flexible and open to adjusting financial plans in response to changing circumstances can enhance resilience. c. **Skill Development:** Acquiring new skills or pursuing educational opportunities can lead to increased earning potential. d. **Diversification:** Exploring multiple income streams and investments can enhance financial security. e. **Self-Care:** Prioritizing physical and mental well-being through exercise, relaxation techniques, and mindfulness reduces the impact of stress.

Financial stress is a reality faced by many individuals, but it need not define one's well-being. By understanding the sources and impact of financial stress, and by implementing practical strategies for managing it, individuals can foster resilience, regain a sense of control, and lead a fulfilling life even in the face of economic challenges. Empowerment, education, and a positive mindset form the foundation for navigating financial stress and emerging stronger on the other side.

Stress management global professional organizations

There are several professional organizations that focus on stress management, mental health, and well-being. These organizations provide resources, support, and education for professionals working in the field of stress management and mental health. Here are a few prominent ones:

- **American Institute of Stress (AIS):** Website: www.stress.org[1] AIS is a non-profit organization that aims to advance the understanding of stress and its impact on health through research, education, and advocacy. It provides resources, publications, and information on stress management techniques.

- **International Stress Management Association (ISMA):** Website: www.isma.org.uk[2] ISMA is a global organization dedicated to promoting the prevention and reduction of stress. It offers training, conferences, and resources for stress management professionals and individuals interested in stress reduction.

- **Association for Applied Psychophysiology and Biofeedback (AAPB):** Website: www.aapb.org[3] AAPB focuses on the application of biofeedback and

---

1. https://www.stress.org/

2. https://www.isma.org.uk/

3. https://www.aapb.org/

psychophysiology for improving health and well-being. It offers educational resources, conferences, and networking opportunities for professionals interested in stress management and biofeedback techniques.

- **National Wellness Institute (NWI):** Website: www.nationalwellness.org[4] NWI is a leading organization in the wellness field, covering various aspects of well-being, including stress management. It provides education, resources, and certifications for wellness professionals and organizations.

- **American Psychological Association (APA):** Website: www.apa.org[5] While not solely focused on stress management, APA is a well-known organization for psychology professionals. It offers resources, publications, and information on mental health and stress-related topics.

- **American Institute for Cognitive Therapy (AICT):** Website: www.cognitivetherapynyc.com[6] AICT focuses on cognitive behavioural therapy (CBT) and related approaches for addressing stress, anxiety, and other mental health concerns. It offers training and resources for mental health professionals.

- **Mindfulness-Based Stress Reduction (MBSR) programs:** Organizations such as the Centre for Mindfulness in Medicine, Health Care, and Society at the University of Massachusetts Medical School offer MBSR programs and training for professionals interested in mindfulness-based stress reduction techniques.

- **Employee Assistance Professionals Association (EAPA):** Website: www.eapassn.org[7] EAPA focuses on the well-being

---

4. https://www.nationalwellness.org/

5. https://www.apa.org/

6. http://www.cognitivetherapynyc.com/

of employees and provides resources and support for Employee Assistance Program (EAP) professionals, who often deal with workplace stress and mental health concerns.

These organizations offer valuable resources, education, networking, and support for professionals working in stress management, mental health, and related fields. Joining such organizations can provide access to the latest research, best practices, and a community of like-minded professionals.

---

7. https://www.eapassn.org/

Stress management organizations in India

C ertainly, here are some stress management and mental health professional organizations in India:

- **Indian Association of Clinical Psychologists (IACP):** Website: www.iacp.in[1] IACP is a professional organization that promotes the field of clinical psychology in India. It provides a platform for psychologists and mental health professionals to exchange knowledge and enhance their skills.
- **Indian Association for Cognitive Therapy (IACT):** Website: www.iact.org.in[2] IACT focuses on cognitive behavioural therapy (CBT) and related approaches for psychological well-being. It offers training, workshops, and resources for professionals interested in evidence-based therapies.
- **Association of Clinical Psychologists (ACP):** Website: www.associationofclinicalpsychologists.org[3] ACP is a body of clinical psychologists in India that provides a platform for networking, professional development, and sharing research findings.
- **Indian Association of Positive Psychology (IAPP):** Website: www.indianassociationofpositivepsychology.org[4]

---

1. http://www.iacp.in/

2. http://www.iact.org.in/

3. http://www.associationofclinicalpsychologists.org/

IAPP promotes the study and application of positive psychology in India. It offers conferences, workshops, and resources for individuals interested in positive psychology interventions and stress management.

- **Indian Psychiatric Society (IPS):** Website: www.indianpsychiatricsociety.org[5] IPS is a professional organization for psychiatrists and mental health professionals. While not exclusively focused on stress management, it covers various aspects of mental health.

- **Wellness and Stress Management Institute (WSMI):** Website: www.stressmanagementindia.org[6] WSMI is dedicated to promoting stress management and wellness. It offers training programs, workshops, and resources for professionals and individuals seeking to manage stress effectively.

- **Indian Association for Social Psychiatry (IASP):** Website: www.indiansocialpsychiatry.org[7] IASP focuses on the interface between psychiatry and society. It provides a forum for mental health professionals to address social and community-related factors affecting mental well-being.

- **National Academy of Psychology (NAOP):** Website: www.naopindia.org[8] NAOP promotes the advancement of psychological research and practice in India. It brings together psychologists and researchers to collaborate on various psychological issues, including stress management.

---

4. http://www.indianassociationofpositivepsychology.org/

5. http://www.indianpsychiatricsociety.org/

6. http://www.stressmanagementindia.org/

7. http://www.indiansocialpsychiatry.org/

8. http://www.naopindia.org/

These organizations offer opportunities for networking, professional development, knowledge sharing, and collaboration among mental health and stress management professionals in India. Joining these associations can provide access to the latest research, training, and a supportive community.

Yoga

Yoga is a holistic system that originated in ancient India and encompasses physical postures (asanas), breathing techniques (pranayama), meditation, and ethical principles. It aims to promote overall well-being by fostering harmony between the body, mind, and spirit. Yoga is not just a physical exercise; it's a way of life that offers numerous physical, mental, and emotional benefits.

Yoga is highly adaptable and can be practiced by individuals of all ages and fitness levels. Whether you're seeking physical fitness, stress relief, or a deeper spiritual connection, incorporating yoga into your routine can have profound and positive effects on your well-being. It's advisable to start with beginner-friendly classes and consult a qualified yoga instructor, especially if you have specific health considerations.

Yoga is a holistic and effective approach for managing stress. It combines physical postures, breathing exercises, meditation, and mindfulness to promote relaxation, reduce tension, and improve overall well-being. Regular practice of yoga can help individuals cope with stress by calming the mind, relaxing the body, and enhancing self-awareness. Here are some key yoga techniques for stress management:

Asanas (Physical Postures):

Gentle and restorative yoga poses can help release physical tension and promote relaxation. Poses like Child's Pose, Forward Fold, and Corpse Pose (Shavasana) are particularly soothing.

Pranayama (Breath Control):

Breathing exercises such as Deep Breathing, Alternate Nostril Breathing (Nadi Shodhana), and 4-7-8 breathing can help calm the nervous system and reduce stress.

Mindfulness Meditation:

Mindful awareness of the present moment can help alleviate stress. Practice sitting or lying down comfortably, focusing on your breath, bodily sensations, or a specific point of focus.

Yoga Nidra:

Also known as yogic sleep, Yoga Nidra is a guided relaxation technique that induces a state of deep relaxation and helps release tension from the body and mind.

Progressive Muscle Relaxation:

This involves tensing and then releasing different muscle groups in the body, helping to release physical tension and promoting relaxation.

Guided Imagery:

Visualization techniques involve imagining peaceful and calming scenes, helping to reduce stress and create a sense of tranquillity.

Vinyasa Flow Yoga:

This dynamic style of yoga combines movement with breath. Flowing through sequences of poses can help alleviate physical tension and bring a sense of focus.

Restorative Yoga:

Restorative poses involve supported postures using props like bolsters and blankets. They encourage deep relaxation and comfort.

Yoga for Flexibility:

Gentle stretching and poses that enhance flexibility can release physical tension and promote a sense of relaxation.

Self-Compassion Practice:

Yoga teaches self-compassion and self-care. By being kind to yourself and treating your body and mind with love and patience, you can reduce stress.

Yoga for Better Sleep:

A regular yoga practice can improve sleep quality by calming the mind and relaxing the body. Evening practices that focus on restorative poses and deep breathing can be particularly helpful.

Yoga Classes and Online Resources:

Joining a yoga class or using online resources (videos, apps, websites) tailored for stress management can provide guidance and structure to your practice.

Traveling

Traveling can indeed be an effective way to relieve stress and rejuvenate the mind, body, and spirit. Taking a break from your daily routine, exploring new places, and engaging in different activities can provide a refreshing change of pace and perspective. Here's how traveling can help you find stress relief:

- **Change of Environment:** Stepping away from your usual surroundings and immersing yourself in a new environment can help break the cycle of stress and routine. Different sights, sounds, and experiences can stimulate your senses and shift your focus.
- **Rest and Relaxation:** Traveling allows you to disconnect from work and responsibilities, giving you the opportunity to rest, relax, and recharge. You can take naps, sleep in, or simply lounge without the usual pressures.
- **Adventures and Exploration:** Engaging in new activities such as hiking, sightseeing, or trying local cuisine can provide a sense of adventure and excitement, taking your mind off stressors.
- **Mindfulness and Present Moment:** Being in a new place encourages you to be present and mindful, as you take in the surroundings and fully experience each moment.
- **Physical Activity:** Traveling often involves walking, exploring, and being more active than usual. Physical activity releases endorphins, which are natural stress reducers.

- **Cultural Exposure:** Experiencing new cultures, traditions, and lifestyles can broaden your horizons and provide a fresh perspective on life, reducing feelings of stress.
- **Quality Time with Loved Ones:** Traveling with family or friends allows you to bond and create cherished memories, enhancing your emotional well-being.
- **Digital Detox:** Traveling can provide an opportunity to disconnect from digital devices and reduce exposure to work-related stressors.
- **Restorative Nature:** Visiting natural landscapes, beaches, or mountains can have a calming effect on the mind and promote relaxation.
- **Social Interaction:** Engaging with locals and fellow travellers can offer social interaction and a sense of belonging.
- **Time for Reflection:** Traveling provides solitude for introspection, helping you gain clarity on your priorities and values.
- **Reduced Decision-Making:** Being in a different environment often means fewer day-to-day decisions to make, allowing your mind to relax.

It's important to plan your trip mindfully, considering factors such as destination, budget, and activities that genuinely bring you joy. While traveling can offer stress relief, it's also essential to manage expectations and not add undue pressure to the experience. If you're unable to travel extensively, even short getaways or day trips can provide similar benefits. Remember that the goal is to create an experience that supports your well-being and helps you return to your routine with a refreshed mindset.

Entertainment

Engaging in entertainment activities can be an excellent way to relieve stress and unwind. Taking time to enjoy activities you love can help shift your focus away from stressors and provide much-needed relaxation. Here are various forms of entertainment that can help you find stress relief:

- **Reading:** Escape into the world of books, whether fiction, non-fiction, or self-help. Reading can transport you to different realms and take your mind off stress.

- **Watching Movies or TV Shows:** Enjoying a movie or binge-watching your favourite TV shows can be a great way to relax and unwind.

- **Listening to Music:** Listen to your favourite music, calming melodies, or upbeat tunes. Music has a powerful impact on mood and can help alleviate stress.

- **Artistic Expression:** Engage in creative activities like drawing, painting, colouring, or crafting. These activities can be meditative and provide a creative outlet.

- **Playing Musical Instruments:** If you play a musical instrument, spending time playing music can be both enjoyable and therapeutic.

- **Cooking or Baking:** Experimenting with new recipes or creating comforting meals and treats can be a delightful way to reduce stress.

- **Gardening:** Spending time in nature, tending to plants, and working in a garden can provide a sense of relaxation and connection with the outdoors.

- **Puzzles and Games:** Solving puzzles, playing board games, or engaging in video games can be engrossing and divert your mind from stressors.
- **Physical Activities:** Engage in physical entertainment such as dancing, yoga, swimming, or going for a walk. Exercise releases endorphins that improve mood.
- **Mindfulness and Meditation Apps:** Use apps specifically designed for relaxation, mindfulness, and meditation to guide you through calming exercises.
- **Comedy and Laughter:** Watching stand-up comedy or engaging in activities that make you laugh can significantly reduce stress.
- **Online Communities and Forums:** Participate in online discussions, forums, or social media groups related to your hobbies or interests. Connecting with like-minded people can be enjoyable and uplifting.
- **Virtual Tours and Experiences:** Explore virtual tours of museums, galleries, or travel destinations from the comfort of your home.
- **Journaling:** Write in a journal to express your thoughts, feelings, and experiences. This can help you process emotions and gain clarity.
- **Photography:** Take up photography and capture moments that bring you joy. This can help you focus on the beauty around you.

The key is to engage in activities that resonate with you and bring you joy. Tailor your entertainment choices to your preferences and schedule. Incorporating regular moments of entertainment into your routine can contribute to a balanced and stress-free lifestyle.

Ayurveda

Ayurveda, an ancient holistic system of medicine originating in India, offers a comprehensive approach to managing stress by balancing the mind, body, and spirit. It focuses on promoting overall well-being through personalized lifestyle practices, dietary choices, herbal remedies, and mindfulness techniques. Here are some Ayurvedic principles and practices for stress management:

- **Identify Your Dosha:** Ayurveda classifies individuals into three doshas (mind-body types): Vata, Pitta, and Kapha. Understanding your dominant dosha can help tailor stress management strategies to your unique constitution.
- **Balanced Diet:** Eat a balanced and nourishing diet that includes fresh, seasonal, and whole foods. Favor foods that pacify your dominant dosha, and minimize foods that exacerbate it. Focus on incorporating nourishing and calming foods.
- **Herbal Remedies:** Ayurveda recommends specific herbs that have adaptogenic and calming properties to support the nervous system. Ashwagandha, Brahmi (Bacopa), and Tulsi (Holy Basil) are commonly used for stress relief.
- **Oil Massage (Abhyanga):** Regular self-massage with warm oil helps promote relaxation, improve circulation, and soothe the nervous system. Use oils suitable for your dosha.
- **Yoga and Pranayama:** Engage in gentle yoga asanas and pranayama (breathing exercises) tailored to your dosha. These

practices help balance energy, reduce tension, and calm the mind.

- **Mindful Eating:** Eat in a calm and mindful manner, savouring each bite. Avoid eating when stressed or distracted, as it can disrupt digestion.
- **Meditation and Mindfulness:** Practice meditation, mindfulness, or deep breathing exercises to quiet the mind, reduce stress, and enhance self-awareness.
- **Adequate Sleep:** Prioritize getting sufficient sleep, as proper rest is essential for balancing the doshas and managing stress.
- **Daily Routine (Dinacharya):** Follow a daily routine that includes waking up and going to bed at consistent times, regular meals, and other self-care practices.
- **Limit Stimulants:** Reduce or avoid stimulants like caffeine, as they can exacerbate stress and disrupt your doshic balance.
- **Ayurvedic Teas:** Sip calming Ayurvedic teas made from herbs like chamomile, ginger, and licoricey to promote relaxation.
- **Aromatherapy:** Use soothing aromas through essential oils like lavender, sandalwood, and frankincense to create a calming environment.
- **Nature Connection:** Spend time in nature to ground yourself and connect with the healing energy of the natural world.
- **Digital Detox:** Set boundaries with digital devices to reduce sensory overload and promote relaxation.
- **Consult an Ayurvedic Practitioner:** Consider consulting an Ayurvedic practitioner to receive personalized guidance based on your dosha and specific stress-related concerns.

Ayurveda emphasizes the interconnectedness of mind, body, and spirit, and its holistic approach to stress management aims to address the root causes of stress while promoting overall well-being. Keep in mind that Ayurveda is a personalized system, and what works best for one person may differ for another. It's recommended to consult an Ayurvedic practitioner before making significant changes to your lifestyle or incorporating new practices.

Balanced Diet

A balanced and nourishing diet plays a crucial role in managing stress by providing your body with the nutrients it needs to support overall well-being and resilience. Certain foods are known to have calming and mood-enhancing effects, while others should be consumed in moderation to avoid exacerbating stress. Here's a dietary guide for stress relief:

Foods to Include:

- **Complex Carbohydrates:** Whole grains like brown rice, quinoa, oats, and whole wheat are rich in fibre and promote stable blood sugar levels, helping to regulate mood.

- **Lean Proteins:** Include sources of lean protein such as poultry, fish, tofu, legumes, and nuts. Protein helps maintain steady energy levels and supports brain function.

- **Omega-3 Fatty Acids:** Found in fatty fish (salmon, mackerel, sardines), flaxseeds, chia seeds, and walnuts, omega-3s have anti-inflammatory properties and support brain health.

- **Leafy Greens:** Spinach, kale, and other leafy greens are rich in magnesium, which can have a calming effect on the nervous system.

- **Nuts and Seeds:** Almonds, walnuts, sunflower seeds, and pumpkin seeds are sources of healthy fats and nutrients that support mood regulation.

- **Fruits and Berries:** Berries, citrus fruits, and other colourful fruits are high in antioxidants and vitamins that promote overall health.

- **Herbal Teas:** Chamomile, lavender, and passionflower teas are known for their calming properties and can help you unwind.

- **Probiotic-Rich Foods:** Yogurt, kefir, sauerkraut, and kimchi support gut health, which is linked to mood and stress management.

- **Dark Chocolate:** Dark chocolate with a high cocoa content can have mood-boosting effects due to its antioxidants and potential to release endorphins.
- **Avocado:** Avocado is rich in healthy fats and contains potassium, which helps regulate blood pressure and supports relaxation.

Foods to Limit:

- **Caffeine:** Limit caffeine intake from sources like coffee, tea, and energy drinks, as excessive caffeine can increase anxiety and disrupt sleep.
- **Refined Sugars and Sweets:** Processed sugary foods can lead to energy crashes and mood swings. Opt for natural sweeteners like honey or maple syrup in moderation.
- **Processed Foods:** Highly processed foods often contain additives and unhealthy fats that can contribute to inflammation and stress.
- **Alcohol:** While some people may find temporary relief in alcohol, excessive consumption can worsen anxiety and negatively impact sleep.

Healthy Eating Habits:

- **Regular Meals:** Eat balanced meals at consistent times to maintain stable blood sugar levels.
- **Mindful Eating:** Eat slowly, savor each bite, and pay attention to hunger and fullness cues.
- **Stay Hydrated:** Drink plenty of water throughout the day to support overall health and well-being.
- **Plan and Prepare:** Plan your meals ahead of time to avoid relying on unhealthy options when stressed.
- **Avoid Emotional Eating:** Be mindful of eating in response to emotions; find alternative ways to manage stress.
- **Variety and Moderation:** Include a variety of nutrient-rich foods in your diet and practice moderation.

Remember that dietary needs can vary from person to person, and it's important to listen to your body and make choices that support your well-being. If you have specific dietary concerns or health conditions, consider consulting a registered dietitian or healthcare professional for personalized guidance.

Findings in stress management

Here are some potential areas of new research and trends in stress management that were gaining attention:

- **Digital Interventions:** Researchers were exploring the effectiveness of digital platforms, mobile apps, and online programs for delivering stress management interventions. These tools often combined cognitive behavioural techniques, mindfulness practices, and relaxation exercises accessible to individuals remotely.

- **Mind-Body Interventions:** Studies were investigating the impact of mind-body practices such as yoga, tai chi, and qigong on stress reduction. These practices integrate physical movement, breathing, and mindfulness to promote relaxation and well-being.

- **Neuroscience and Brain-Computer Interfaces:** Advancements in neuroimaging and brain-computer interfaces were allowing researchers to better understand the neural mechanisms of stress and develop personalized interventions based on brain activity patterns.

- **Epigenetics and Stress:** Research was delving into the field of epigenetics, which explores how stress and environmental factors can influence gene expression. Understanding these interactions could lead to targeted stress management strategies.

- **Resilience and Positive Psychology:** Studies were focusing on enhancing resilience through positive psychology interventions, emphasizing strengths, gratitude, and optimism to better cope with stressors.

- **Nutritional Approaches:** Researchers were investigating the impact of nutrition and dietary interventions on stress management. Specific nutrients and dietary patterns were being studied for their potential to influence stress hormones and mood.

- **Employer-Based Programs:** Workplace stress was gaining attention, with research focusing on the development and evaluation of stress management programs within organizational settings. These programs aimed to improve employee well-being and performance.

- **Virtual Reality (VR) and Augmented Reality (AR):** VR and AR technologies were being explored as tools for creating immersive and controlled environments to manage stress and anxiety.

- **Social Support and Community Interventions:** Research was highlighting the role of social support networks and community-based interventions in buffering against the negative effects of stress. Group activities and peer support were examined.

- **Cultural and Diversity Considerations:** Studies were recognizing the importance of culturally sensitive stress management approaches that acknowledge how different cultural backgrounds and identities can influence stress experiences and coping strategies.

- **Ecotherapy and Nature-Based Interventions:** Researchers were exploring the therapeutic benefits of spending time in nature, with studies showing that exposure to natural environments can have a positive impact on stress reduction and mental well-being.

- **Biometric and Wearable Devices:** Wearable devices with biometric sensors were being studied for their potential to provide real-time feedback on stress levels and promote self-regulation.

Remember that the field of stress management is dynamic, and new research is constantly emerging. To access the latest information, consider searching scientific journals, academic databases, and reputable research institutions' websites for the most recent findings and trends in stress management.

Helping stressed person

Supporting a stressed person requires empathy, patience, and understanding. Here are some steps you can take to help someone who is stressed:

- **Listen:** Give them your full attention and let them share their thoughts and feelings. Sometimes, just having someone to talk to can be immensely comforting.
- **Be Empathetic:** Show that you understand and care about their feelings. Avoid minimizing their stress or comparing it to others' experiences.
- **Offer a Safe Space:** Create an environment where they feel comfortable opening up without fear of judgment.
- **Ask How You Can Help:** Offer your assistance but also ask what specific support they need. People cope differently, so their preferences may vary.
- **Provide Practical Help:** Offer assistance with tasks that might be causing stress, such as running errands or helping with chores.
- **Encourage Self-Care:** Remind them to prioritize self-care activities that help reduce stress, such as exercise, relaxation techniques, and spending time in nature.
- **Share Resources:** Provide information on stress management techniques, mindfulness practices, or professional help options if they're open to it.
- **Offer Distractions:** Sometimes engaging in a pleasant

activity together, like watching a movie or going for a walk, can help take their mind off stressors.

- **Avoid Adding Pressure:** Don't push them to talk or share more than they're comfortable with. Let them control the pace.
- **Stay Patient:** Stress doesn't always resolve quickly. Continue to be supportive even if their stress continues for some time.
- **Validate Their Feelings:** Let them know that their feelings are valid and that it's okay to feel stressed.
- **Check In Regularly:** Continue to be there for them over time. Staying in touch shows that you genuinely care.
- **Respect Their Privacy:** If they prefer to handle their stress alone, respect their decision while still offering your support.
- **Encourage Professional Help:** If their stress seems overwhelming or persistent, suggest they consider talking to a mental health professional.
- **Model Healthy Coping:** By practicing healthy stress management yourself, you can be a positive example and encourage them to do the same.

Remember that everyone's needs are unique, so tailor your support to their individual preferences. Additionally, if you're concerned about their safety or well-being, don't hesitate to reach out for professional help or involve a mental health expert.

Digital Interventions in Stress management

Digital interventions in stress management leverage technology to provide accessible and convenient ways for individuals to manage and reduce stress. These interventions can include mobile apps, online platforms, wearable devices, and virtual reality experiences that offer a range of tools and techniques to promote relaxation, mindfulness, and overall well-being. Here are some common types of digital interventions in stress management:

- **Mindfulness and Meditation Apps:** These apps provide guided meditation sessions, breathing exercises, and mindfulness practices. They help users focus their attention, reduce anxiety, and improve their ability to manage stress.
- **Stress Tracking Apps:** These apps allow users to track their stress levels, identify triggers, and monitor their progress over time. They may also provide insights into how lifestyle factors affect stress.
- **Relaxation and Breathing Exercises:** Many apps offer interactive tools for deep breathing and progressive muscle relaxation, helping users to calm their minds and bodies.
- **Biofeedback Devices and Apps:** Wearable devices equipped with sensors can monitor physiological indicators of stress, such as heart rate variability and skin conductance. Connected apps provide real-time feedback and suggest interventions to regulate stress responses.

- **Virtual Reality (VR) Experiences:** VR applications create immersive environments that help users escape from stressors and engage in relaxing scenarios, such as nature walks or calming landscapes.
- **Online Mindfulness Programs:** These web-based platforms offer structured mindfulness courses, video lessons, and interactive activities to teach stress reduction techniques.
- **Cognitive Behavioural Therapy (CBT) Apps:** CBT-based apps provide techniques to reframe negative thoughts, manage stressors, and develop healthier coping strategies.
- **Digital Relaxation Tools:** Apps and websites offer audio tracks with soothing sounds, music, or nature sounds to create a calming atmosphere.
- **Guided Imagery and Visualization Apps:** These apps provide guided sessions that help users create positive mental images to reduce stress and anxiety.
- **Sleep-Enhancing Apps:** Quality sleep is essential for stress management. Sleep-focused apps offer techniques to improve sleep hygiene and relaxation before bedtime.
- **Social Support Platforms:** Online communities and forums connect individuals experiencing stress, providing a space to share experiences, gain insights, and receive support.
- **Chatbots and AI-Powered Apps:** Some apps use artificial intelligence to engage users in conversations, offering emotional support, coping strategies, and resources.
- **Digital Journals and Reflection Apps:** Writing about stressors, emotions, and gratitude can be therapeutic. Digital journaling apps make it easy to track thoughts and feelings.
- **Daily Affirmations and Positive Reminders:** Apps deliver positive affirmations and reminders to encourage a positive mindset and reduce stress.
- **Biometric Wearables:** Wearable devices equipped with

stress-tracking features monitor physiological indicators and offer personalized suggestions for stress reduction.

Digital interventions provide the flexibility to manage stress on the go and at your own pace. However, it's important to choose reputable apps and platforms that are evidence-based and designed by qualified professionals. Additionally, while digital tools can be helpful, they should not replace professional mental health support when needed.

Epigenetics and Stress

Epigenetics is the study of changes in gene expression that do not involve alterations to the DNA sequence itself. These changes can be influenced by various environmental factors, including stress. Epigenetic modifications can have a significant impact on how genes are activated or silenced, ultimately affecting an individual's health and well-being. When it comes to stress, epigenetics plays a crucial role in understanding how external factors can influence our biology and contribute to various health outcomes.

Here's how epigenetics and stress are connected:

- **Stress-Induced Epigenetic Changes:** Stressors, whether acute or chronic, can trigger epigenetic changes. These changes can affect gene expression patterns and contribute to various physiological and psychological responses associated with stress.
- **DNA Methylation:** One common epigenetic modification is DNA methylation, where a methyl group is added to the DNA molecule. Stress has been linked to alterations in DNA methylation patterns, which can impact the expression of genes related to stress response, inflammation, and other biological processes.
- **Histone Modifications:** Histones are proteins around which DNA is wound. Epigenetic modifications of histones can affect how tightly DNA is packaged and thus influence gene accessibility. Stress can lead to changes in histone

modifications that impact gene expression.

- **Non-Coding RNAs:** Epigenetics also involves non-coding RNAs, which are molecules that regulate gene expression. Stress can influence the levels of certain non-coding RNAs, which in turn affect how genes are transcribed.

- **Transgenerational Effects:** Some epigenetic changes induced by stress can be passed down to offspring. This concept is known as transgenerational epigenetic inheritance and suggests that the impact of stress on gene expression may extend beyond the individual experiencing the stress.

- **Health Implications:** Epigenetic changes due to stress can influence various health outcomes. For instance, chronic stress-related epigenetic alterations might contribute to conditions such as cardiovascular diseases, mental health disorders, and metabolic disorders.

- **Resilience and Vulnerability:** Epigenetic modifications can play a role in why some individuals are more resilient to stress while others are more vulnerable. Genetic predisposition interacts with environmental factors, including stress, to influence an individual's stress response and overall well-being.

- **Personalized Medicine:** Understanding epigenetic changes in response to stress can contribute to the development of personalized approaches to stress management and healthcare. By considering an individual's epigenetic profile, interventions can be tailored to their specific needs.

- **Reversibility:** Epigenetic changes are reversible to some extent. This means that lifestyle interventions, such as stress reduction techniques, healthy diet, exercise, and mindfulness practices, can potentially reverse or mitigate stress-induced epigenetic modifications.

It's important to note that while research has revealed the connection between stress and epigenetics, the field is complex and still being explored. Many factors contribute to an individual's response to stress and the resulting epigenetic changes. Additionally, ongoing research aims to uncover more specific mechanisms and potential interventions to manage the epigenetic effects of stress and improve overall well-being.

Neuroscience and Brain-Computer Interfaces

Neuroscience and brain-computer interfaces (BCIs) are areas of research that offer insights into how the brain functions and how technology can be used to interact with and influence brain activity. These fields have significant implications for understanding and managing stress. Here's how neuroscience and brain-computer interfaces are relevant to stress:

- **Stress Response in the Brain:** Neuroscience studies have revealed the brain regions and neural pathways involved in the stress response. The amygdala and the hypothalamus-pituitary-adrenal (HPA) axis play crucial roles in triggering and regulating stress reactions.

- **Neuroplasticity:** Neuroscience research demonstrates the brain's ability to change and adapt, known as neuroplasticity. This implies that stress-related changes in brain structure and function can potentially be reversed or modified through interventions.

- **Neurofeedback:** Neurofeedback is a technique that utilizes real-time brain activity data to help individuals regulate their own brain functions. It can be used to train individuals to manage stress by increasing activity in areas associated with relaxation and reducing activity in stress-related regions.

- **Mindfulness and Meditation:** Neuroscience studies have shown that mindfulness and meditation practices can lead to structural and functional changes in the brain. These practices are associated with reduced activity in the amygdala, leading to decreased stress responses.

- **Functional MRI (fMRI):** Functional MRI is used to measure changes in blood flow that indicate brain activity. It's been used to study the impact of stress on brain activity and to identify neural pathways involved in stress regulation.

- **EEG and Brainwaves:** Electroencephalography (EEG) measures brainwave activity. Certain EEG patterns are associated with relaxation and reduced stress. Neurofeedback based on EEG can help individuals learn to induce these patterns.

- **Cortisol Regulation:** Neuroscience studies have explored how stress influences cortisol production. Cortisol, a stress hormone, can impact brain function and overall well-being.

- **Brain-Computer Interfaces (BCIs):** BCIs are devices that allow direct communication between the brain and external devices. While often associated with medical applications, BCIs could potentially be used for stress management. For instance, BCIs might be used to trigger relaxation responses through neurofeedback or virtual reality experiences.

- **Virtual Reality (VR) and Stress Exposure Therapy:** Neuroscience research supports the effectiveness of VR-based stress exposure therapy. VR environments can simulate stressors and help individuals confront and manage stress-related triggers in a controlled setting.

- **Neuroinflammation:** Chronic stress can lead to neuroinflammation, which affects brain health. Understanding the neuroinflammatory processes involved can lead to targeted interventions.

- **Resilience Training:** Neuroscience studies investigate the neural mechanisms underlying resilience and how training can enhance an individual's ability to cope with stress.

- **Pharmacological Interventions:** Neuroscience research contributes to the development of medications targeting neurotransmitter systems involved in stress and anxiety regulation.

Combining neuroscience insights with technology like brain-computer interfaces holds promise for creating personalized stress management approaches. However, it's important to note that the field is still evolving, and ethical considerations must be addressed when dealing with brain data and interventions. Additionally, a multidisciplinary approach involving neuroscientists, psychologists, clinicians, and ethicists is essential to ensure the responsible and effective application of these technologies for stress management.

Cognitive Behavioural Therapy (CBT) Apps

Cognitive Behavioural Therapy (CBT) apps are digital tools designed to provide users with access to CBT-based interventions for managing mental health concerns, including stress, anxiety, depression, and more. CBT is a widely recognized and effective therapeutic approach that helps individuals identify and challenge negative thought patterns and behaviours to improve their emotional well-being. CBT apps offer a convenient way to learn and practice CBT techniques at one's own pace. Here are some features and benefits of CBT apps:

- **Psychoeducation:** CBT apps often provide educational content that explains the principles of CBT, helping users understand how thoughts, emotions, and behaviours are interconnected.

- **Self-Assessment:** Many apps begin with a self-assessment or questionnaire to help users identify their specific challenges and concerns. This information is used to tailor the app's content to individual needs.

- **Goal Setting:** Users can set personalized goals for managing stress and other mental health issues. Apps track progress and celebrate achievements.

- **Thought Monitoring:** CBT apps help users recognize negative thought patterns and track their thoughts throughout the day. This awareness is a key step in challenging and reframing unhelpful thoughts.

- **Behavioural Experiments:** Apps guide users through behavioural experiments, helping them test the validity of their negative beliefs and assumptions.
- **Thought Restructuring:** Users learn techniques to reframe and replace negative thoughts with more balanced and realistic ones.
- **Mindfulness and Relaxation Exercises:** Many CBT apps integrate mindfulness and relaxation exercises to help users manage stress and anxiety.
- **Interactive Tools:** Apps often include interactive tools, such as mood trackers, journaling features, and coping strategies for challenging situations.
- **Guided Exercises:** Users receive step-by-step guidance through CBT exercises, making it easy to practice techniques effectively.
- **Progress Tracking:** Users can track their progress over time, which can be motivating and provide insights into the effectiveness of the interventions.
- **Access to Support:** Some apps offer access to therapists or mental health professionals through messaging or video sessions, enhancing the user's support network.
- **Personalization:** CBT apps can adapt to users' preferences and needs, delivering content and exercises that resonate with their experiences.
- **Privacy and Confidentiality:** Reputable CBT apps prioritize user privacy and data security, creating a safe space for users to explore their thoughts and feelings.
- **Convenience:** CBT apps allow users to practice CBT techniques whenever and wherever they choose, fitting into their schedules.
- **Cost-Effectiveness:** Many CBT apps are more affordable

than traditional therapy and can be a valuable supplement to face-to-face sessions.

It's important to choose CBT apps developed by reputable sources, such as licensed therapists, mental health organizations, or institutions. Look for apps with positive user reviews, evidence-based content, and a clear privacy policy. While CBT apps can be a helpful tool, they are not a replacement for professional treatment. If you're dealing with severe stress or mental health issues, consider consulting a mental health professional for personalized guidance and support.

Sleep-Enhancing Apps

Sleep-enhancing apps are designed to help individuals improve the quality and duration of their sleep. These apps offer a range of features and techniques to promote better sleep hygiene, relaxation, and overall sleep wellness. Here are some common features and benefits of sleep-enhancing apps:

- **Sleep Tracking:** Many apps monitor and track your sleep patterns, including the time you spend in different sleep stages like REM and deep sleep. This information helps you understand your sleep quality and identify any patterns that might be affecting your sleep.

- **Sleep Diary:** Apps often include a sleep diary feature where you can record details about your daily routines, sleep habits, and any factors that may impact your sleep.

- **Bedtime Reminders:** These apps can set bedtime reminders to establish a consistent sleep schedule, helping you regulate your body's internal clock.

- **Wake-Up Alarms:** Some apps offer smart alarms that wake you up during a light sleep phase, minimizing the grogginess associated with waking up during deep sleep.

- **Relaxation and Breathing Exercises:** Many sleep-enhancing apps include guided relaxation exercises and deep breathing techniques to help you unwind before bedtime.

- **White Noise and Soundscape:** Apps provide calming sounds like white noise, rain, ocean waves, or other soothing sounds that can mask disruptive noises and create a tranquil sleep environment.

- **Sleep Stories:** Some apps offer narrated stories or calming audio content designed to help you relax and drift off to sleep.
- **Mindfulness and Meditation:** Sleep-enhancing apps may include mindfulness and meditation exercises to clear your mind and reduce stress before sleep.
- **Progress Tracking:** These apps allow you to track your sleep progress over time, offering insights into how your sleep habits are improving.
- **Sleep Challenges:** Apps may include challenges or programs that guide you through specific sleep-related goals, such as reducing caffeine intake or limiting screen time before bed.
- **Light and Dark Exposure:** Some apps provide information on how exposure to natural light during the day and limited exposure to artificial light at night can regulate your circadian rhythms.
- **Customizable Environments:** You can often personalize the app settings to create the ideal sleep environment for you, adjusting factors like sound volume and screen brightness.
- **Sleep Science Education:** Many apps provide information about the science of sleep, helping you understand the importance of sleep and how to improve it.
- **Social Jet Lag Detection:** Apps might analyse your sleep patterns to identify discrepancies between your weekday and weekend sleep schedules, which can lead to social jet lag and affect sleep quality.
- **Caffeine and Alcohol Tracking:** Some apps help you track your caffeine and alcohol consumption, as these factors can significantly impact sleep quality.

While sleep-enhancing apps can provide valuable tools and insights, they are not a substitute for addressing underlying sleep disorders or consulting a healthcare professional if you have chronic sleep issues. If you're experiencing persistent sleep problems, it's advisable to consult a medical professional for a comprehensive assessment and personalized recommendations.

Employer-Based Programs for stress management

Employer-based stress management programs are initiatives implemented by companies to promote the well-being of their employees and help them effectively manage workplace stress. These programs are designed to create a healthier work environment, reduce burnout, enhance productivity, and improve overall employee satisfaction. Here are some key components and benefits of employer-based stress management programs:

Components of Employer-Based Stress Management Programs:

- **Wellness Workshops and Seminars:** Companies may offer workshops and seminars on stress management, mindfulness, time management, and other relevant topics. These educational sessions equip employees with practical tools to cope with stress.
- **Physical Activity Initiatives:** Encouraging physical activity through fitness challenges, group exercise classes, or access to on-site gyms can improve employee well-being and help reduce stress.
- **Mental Health Support:** Providing access to Employee Assistance Programs (EAPs), counselling services, or mental health resources can ensure employees have the support they need to manage stress and mental health concerns.
- **Flexible Work Arrangements:** Offering flexible work hours, remote work options, or compressed workweeks can help employees better balance work and personal responsibilities, reducing stress.
- **Workload and Task Management:** Employers can promote effective workload distribution, prioritize tasks, and provide training in time management to prevent employees from feeling overwhelmed.
- **Stress-Reduction Activities:** Offering stress-relief activities like meditation sessions, yoga classes, and relaxation spaces within the workplace can help employees unwind and

recharge.

- **Healthy Nutrition Programs:** Providing healthy food options, nutritional guidance, and workshops on mindful eating can contribute to overall well-being and stress reduction.

- **Communication Channels:** Creating open channels for communication between employees and management can foster a supportive environment where stressors and concerns can be addressed.

- **Workplace Policies:** Developing and enforcing policies that promote work-life balance, prevent overwork, and discourage a culture of excessive stress is essential.

- **Recognition and Rewards:** Recognizing employee achievements and contributions can boost morale and motivation, reducing stress associated with job dissatisfaction.

Benefits of Employer-Based Stress Management Programs:

- **Improved Employee Well-Being:** These programs enhance physical and mental well-being, leading to increased job satisfaction and decreased absenteeism.
- **Increased Productivity:** Employees who are less stressed are generally more focused, engaged, and productive in their roles.
- **Reduced Turnover:** Addressing workplace stress can contribute to higher employee retention rates, as employees are more likely to stay in a supportive and healthy work environment.
- **Enhanced Employee Morale:** Stress management programs demonstrate that employers care about their employees' health and happiness, boosting morale and loyalty.
- **Positive Company Culture:** A focus on well-being and stress management contributes to a positive company culture that values employee health and work-life balance.
- **Cost Savings:** Reducing stress-related health issues and absenteeism can lead to cost savings for employers in the long run.
- **Compliance with Regulations:** Some jurisdictions require employers to address workplace stress as part of health and safety regulations.

Employer-based stress management programs are most effective when they are comprehensive, tailored to the specific needs of the workforce, and integrated into the company's overall wellness strategy. Regular assessments and feedback from employees can help companies refine and improve these programs over time.

Cortisol Regulation

Cortisol is a hormone produced by the adrenal glands in response to stress. It's often referred to as the "stress hormone" because its levels increase in times of stress or when the body perceives a threat. Cortisol plays a crucial role in the body's fight-or-flight response, which prepares the body to respond to challenges. However, chronic stress can lead to dysregulation of cortisol levels, which can have negative health effects. Effective stress management includes strategies to regulate cortisol levels. Here's how cortisol regulation is connected to stress management:

- **Understanding the Cortisol Response:** In a stressor situation, the body releases cortisol to mobilize energy and resources to handle the threat. This response is beneficial in short-term situations but can become problematic when stress is chronic.

- **Chronic Stress and Cortisol Dysregulation:** Prolonged exposure to stressors, such as work pressure, relationship issues, or financial worries, can lead to chronically elevated cortisol levels. This dysregulation can contribute to various health issues, including anxiety, depression, weight gain, sleep disturbances, and weakened immune function.

- **Importance of Cortisol Balance:** Effective stress management aims to maintain a healthy balance of cortisol levels. This involves both reducing chronic stressors and employing strategies to regulate cortisol release.

- **Stress Reduction Techniques:** Techniques such as mindfulness meditation, deep breathing, progressive muscle relaxation, and yoga have been shown to help regulate cortisol levels by activating the body's relaxation response.
- **Physical Activity:** Regular exercise can help manage stress and cortisol levels. Engaging in aerobic exercise and physical activities you enjoy can reduce stress and promote a healthy cortisol response.
- **Healthy Sleep Patterns:** Consistent and quality sleep is essential for cortisol regulation. Poor sleep or disrupted sleep patterns can contribute to cortisol dysregulation and exacerbate stress.
- **Balanced Nutrition:** A balanced diet with adequate nutrients, including complex carbohydrates, lean proteins, and healthy fats, can support cortisol regulation. Avoiding excessive sugar and caffeine intake can also help.
- **Social Support:** Maintaining strong social connections and a supportive network can buffer against the negative effects of stress on cortisol levels.
- **Mindful Eating:** Practicing mindful eating can help regulate cortisol by promoting a balanced approach to food and reducing stress-related emotional eating.
- **Stress Management Techniques:** Incorporating stress management techniques into your routine, such as time management, setting realistic goals, and using effective problem-solving strategies, can reduce chronic stress and its impact on cortisol.
- **Nature and Relaxation:** Spending time in nature, engaging in hobbies, and participating in relaxation activities can all contribute to cortisol regulation.
- **Limiting Stimulants:** Limiting or moderating caffeine intake and avoiding excessive use of stimulants can help

prevent cortisol spikes.

Remember that cortisol regulation is just one aspect of stress management. Effective stress management involves a holistic approach that addresses physical, emotional, and psychological aspects of stress. If you find it challenging to manage stress on your own, consider seeking support from a healthcare professional or mental health expert.

soothing music for stress relief

Soothing music can be incredibly effective for stress relief and relaxation. Music has the power to influence our mood and physiology, helping to calm the mind, reduce anxiety, and promote a sense of well-being. Here are some types of soothing music that you might find beneficial for stress relief:

- **Classical Music:** Classical compositions with gentle melodies and slower tempos can have a soothing effect. Pieces by composers like Johann Pachelbel, Claude Debussy, and Ludwig van Beethoven are often used for relaxation.

- **Nature Sounds and Ambient Music:** Music combined with sounds of nature, such as flowing water, chirping birds, or gentle rain, can create a calming atmosphere reminiscent of natural settings.

- **Piano and Instrumental Music:** Solo piano music or instrumental tracks featuring instruments like the flute, violin, or harp can create a serene and peaceful ambiance.

- **Binaural Beats:** Binaural beats are a type of sound therapy that involves playing two slightly different frequencies in each ear. They are believed to influence brainwave patterns and induce relaxation.

- **Chill-out and Downtempo:** Modern electronic music genres like chill-out and downtempo often feature laid-back beats and ambient sounds, providing a soothing backdrop for relaxation.

- **New Age and Spa Music:** New Age music and spa-inspired compositions are designed specifically for relaxation, often incorporating soft melodies, calming textures, and gentle rhythms.
- **Guided Meditation and Yoga Music:** Music designed for guided meditation, deep breathing exercises, or yoga practice can help you enter a state of relaxation and mindfulness.
- **Celtic and Folk Music:** Melodies from Celtic or folk traditions can create a sense of tranquillity, evoking a connection to nature and cultural heritage.
- **Guitar and Acoustic Music:** Acoustic guitar or other string instrument melodies can be soothing and evoke feelings of comfort.
- **Movie and Soundtrack Scores:** Soundtracks from movies and TV shows, especially those with emotive and gentle themes, can have a calming effect.

When using music for stress relief, it's important to create a comfortable environment where you can focus on the music without distractions. You can listen to soothing music while practicing relaxation techniques, meditating, taking a warm bath, or simply lying down with your eyes closed. Experiment with different types of music to find what resonates with you the most. Remember that individual preferences vary, so choose music that you personally find calming and enjoyable.

spa therapy for stress management

Spa therapy, also known as spa treatments or spa relaxation, is a holistic approach to stress management that combines various therapeutic techniques and activities to promote relaxation, rejuvenation, and overall well-being. Spa therapies create an environment where individuals can unwind, disconnect from daily stressors, and focus on self-care. Here are some common spa therapies and activities that can be effective for stress management:

- **Massage Therapy:** Massage involves the manipulation of muscles and soft tissues using various techniques such as Swedish massage, deep tissue massage, and aromatherapy massage. It helps to relieve muscle tension, reduce stress hormones, and promote relaxation.
- **Aromatherapy:** Aromatherapy involves the use of essential oils derived from plants to enhance relaxation and mood. Inhaling or applying these oils during massages or spa treatments can have a calming effect.
- **Hot Stone Therapy:** Warm stones are placed on specific points of the body to relax muscles and improve circulation. The combination of heat and massage can reduce stress and induce a sense of tranquillity.
- **Hydrotherapy:** Hydrotherapy includes treatments like hot tubs, saunas, steam rooms, and hydrotherapy pools. The heat and water stimulate circulation, ease muscle tension, and promote relaxation.
- **Facials:** Facials involve cleansing, exfoliation, and moisturizing of the skin. The pampering experience can have a positive effect on mood and provide a break from daily stress.
- **Body Scrubs and Wraps:** Exfoliating body scrubs and wraps remove dead skin cells and nourish the skin. These treatments can leave you feeling refreshed and rejuvenated.
- **Yoga and Meditation:** Many spas offer yoga and meditation classes in serene environments. These practices help manage stress by promoting mindfulness and relaxation.
- **Tai Chi and Qigong:** These gentle movement practices promote relaxation, balance, and stress reduction through

slow, flowing movements and controlled breathing.

- **Breathing Exercises:** Spa therapists may guide clients through deep breathing exercises that promote relaxation and reduce anxiety.
- **Silence and Solitude:** Some spa facilities offer quiet spaces where guests can disconnect from technology, relax in a serene environment, and enjoy moments of solitude.
- **Healthy Nutrition:** Many spas offer healthy and nourishing meals as part of their packages. A balanced diet can positively impact stress management.
- **Nature and Outdoor Activities:** Spas located in natural settings often provide access to outdoor activities like hiking, walking trails, and nature walks, which can be soothing and refreshing.
- **Creative Workshops:** Some spas offer creative workshops such as art classes or writing sessions, providing a therapeutic outlet for self-expression.
- **Relaxation Lounges:** Relaxation lounges provide comfortable spaces where guests can rest, read, or simply unwind before or after treatments.
- **Digital Detox:** Some spas encourage guests to disconnect from their devices to fully immerse themselves in the spa experience and reduce digital-related stress.

Spa therapy can be an effective way to manage stress and promote overall well-being. Whether you're visiting a spa retreat or creating a spa-like environment at home, the key is to prioritize self-care, relaxation, and mindfulness during the experience.

Sharing thoughts with friends

Sharing your thoughts and feelings with friends can be a valuable way to relieve stress and gain emotional support. Friends often provide a safe space for you to express yourself, receive validation, and receive different perspectives on your challenges. Here are some tips for effectively sharing your thoughts with friends for stress relief:

- **Choose the Right Friend:** Select a friend whom you trust and feel comfortable opening up to. Someone who is empathetic, non-judgmental, and a good listener can be especially helpful.

- **Pick the Right Time and Place:** Find a quiet and comfortable environment where you can have an uninterrupted conversation. Choose a time when both you and your friend are relaxed and able to focus.

- **Be Honest and Open:** Share your thoughts and feelings honestly. Be authentic about what you're experiencing and why you're feeling stressed. Authenticity can foster deeper connections.

- **Practice Active Listening:** When your friend responds, practice active listening by giving them your full attention. This shows respect and validates their input.

- **Be Specific:** Clearly explain the situations or stressors that are bothering you. Providing details helps your friend understand the context and offer more relevant support.

- **Express Your Needs:** Let your friend know what kind of

support you're seeking. Sometimes you might want advice, while other times you may just need someone to listen.

- **Stay Open to Advice:** Be open to the advice and perspectives your friend offers, even if it's different from your own. They may offer insights you hadn't considered.

- **Avoid Judging or Criticizing:** While it's okay to express your frustrations, try to avoid directing negative emotions toward your friend or anyone else. Focus on sharing your feelings without blaming others.

- **Seek Empathy:** Emotional validation is important. A supportive friend can provide empathy and validation for your emotions, making you feel understood and less alone.

- **Set Boundaries:** If a topic becomes too overwhelming or sensitive, don't hesitate to communicate your boundaries and let your friend know if you need a break from the conversation.

- **Maintain Confidentiality:** Make sure your friend knows that what you share is confidential. This encourages trust and creates a safe space for sharing.

- **Return the Favor:** Remember that friendship is a two-way street. Be there for your friend when they need to talk or seek support as well.

- **Express Gratitude:** After sharing your thoughts, express gratitude for your friend's willingness to listen and support you. This shows that you value their friendship.

- **Consider Professional Help:** While friends can provide valuable support, if your stress becomes overwhelming or persistent, consider seeking guidance from a mental health professional.

Sharing your thoughts with friends can be cathartic and help alleviate the burden of stress. It's important to maintain a balance between seeking support from friends and seeking professional help when needed, especially for complex or ongoing stressors.

Meditation for stress relief

Meditation is a powerful practice that can be highly effective for stress relief. It involves training your mind to focus on the present moment, cultivating a sense of mindfulness, and promoting relaxation. Regular meditation practice can help reduce anxiety, enhance emotional well-being, and improve your ability to manage stress. Here's how you can use meditation for stress relief:

- **Choose a Comfortable Environment:** Find a quiet and comfortable space where you won't be easily disturbed. Sit or lie down in a relaxed posture.
- **Set a Time:** Start with a manageable duration, such as 5-10 minutes. As you become more comfortable with meditation, you can gradually increase the time.
- **Focus on Your Breath:** Close your eyes and bring your attention to your breath. Notice the sensation of the breath as you inhale and exhale.
- **Mindfulness of Breath:** Pay attention to each breath without trying to change it. If your mind wanders, gently guide your focus back to your breath.
- **Body Scan:** Progressively move your attention through different parts of your body, noticing any tension or sensations. Release any tension you become aware of.
- **Guided Meditation:** Use guided meditation apps or recordings that provide instructions and visualization to guide you through the process.

- **Mantra Meditation:** Repeat a calming word, phrase, or mantra silently to yourself as you breathe. This can help keep your mind focused.
- **Focus on Sensations:** Shift your attention to physical sensations, such as the feeling of your breath, the warmth of your hands, or the contact with the surface you're sitting on.
- **Accept Your Thoughts:** When thoughts arise, acknowledge them without judgment and then gently return your focus to your chosen point of meditation (breath, mantra, etc.).
- **Progressive Muscle Relaxation:** Tense and then release different muscle groups, one at a time, to release physical tension and promote relaxation.
- **Loving-Kindness Meditation:** Cultivate feelings of compassion and well-wishing towards yourself and others. This can help reduce stress and foster positive emotions.
- **Walking Meditation:** Practice mindful walking by focusing on each step, the sensation of your feet connecting with the ground, and your breath.
- **Consistency:** Regular practice is key. Aim to meditate daily, even if it's for a short duration. Consistency helps reinforce the benefits.
- **Non-Judgment:** Approach meditation with an open mind and without judgment. It's okay if your mind wanders; the practice is about bringing your focus back.
- **Patience:** Be patient with yourself. Meditation is a skill that takes time to develop. Over time, you'll likely notice improvements in your ability to manage stress.

Remember that meditation is a personal practice, and there's no one-size-fits-all approach. Explore different techniques and find what resonates with you. If you're new to meditation, starting with guided meditation apps or classes can provide helpful guidance. With regular practice, you can cultivate a greater sense of calm, mindfulness, and resilience to navigate stress more effectively.

Playing with kids for stress relief

Playing with kids can indeed be a wonderful way to relieve stress and experience a sense of joy and relaxation. Engaging in play activities with children can help you reconnect with your inner child, shift your focus away from stressors, and experience the present moment. Here are some ideas for using playtime with kids as a stress relief technique:

- **Outdoor Play:** Spend time outdoors playing games like tag, hide and seek, soccer, or flying a kite. Fresh air and physical activity can help reduce stress and boost mood.
- **Arts and Crafts:** Engage in creative activities like drawing, painting, making crafts, or building simple DIY projects. These activities encourage mindfulness and creativity.
- **Pretend Play:** Join children in imaginative play scenarios, such as playing house, pretending to be pirates, or acting out stories. Immerse yourself in their world and let go of adult responsibilities for a while.
- **Board Games and Puzzles:** Play board games, card games, or puzzles that are age-appropriate. These activities can be both fun and mentally engaging.
- **Dress-Up and Role Play:** Have a dress-up session where you and the kids can put on costumes and act out different characters or scenarios.
- **Building with Blocks or LEGO:** Building structures together using blocks or LEGO can be a creative and

enjoyable way to bond and alleviate stress.

- **Cooking or Baking:** Involve kids in simple cooking or baking activities. This not only creates a fun experience but also provides opportunities for learning and teamwork.
- **Music and Dancing:** Put on some music and dance together. Dancing is not only physically beneficial but can also be a great way to release stress and have fun.
- **Nature Exploration:** Go on a nature walk, explore the backyard, or visit a park. Observe plants, insects, and animals, and encourage kids' curiosity.
- **Storytelling:** Create and tell stories together. Let your imagination run wild and make up tales with unexpected twists and turns.
- **Yoga for Kids:** Practice kid-friendly yoga poses together. This can be a relaxing and playful way to stretch your body and practice mindfulness.
- **Building Forts:** Use blankets, pillows, and furniture to build indoor forts. Spend time inside your cozy fort reading books, telling stories, or simply relaxing.
- **Water Play:** If weather permits, engage in water play activities like splashing in a kiddie pool, playing with water balloons, or having a water gun fight.
- **Planting and Gardening:** Involve kids in planting flowers or vegetables in the garden or in pots. Connecting with nature can be soothing and rewarding.
- **Unstructured Play:** Sometimes, the best stress relief comes from simply allowing unstructured play. Let kids take the lead and follow their imaginative ideas.

Playing with kids can create special moments of connection and laughter. It's a reminder to be present, playful, and carefree, helping you temporarily escape the pressures of adulthood and experience the simple joys of life.

Planting and Gardening

Planting and gardening can be incredibly therapeutic and effective for stress relief. The act of tending to plants, connecting with nature, and watching your garden flourish can provide a sense of accomplishment, relaxation, and connection with the natural world. Here's how planting and gardening can help with stress relief:

- **Connection with Nature:** Spending time outdoors and interacting with plants allows you to connect with the natural environment, which has been shown to reduce stress and promote well-being.

- **Mindfulness and Presence:** Gardening encourages mindfulness as you focus on the present moment, observing the growth and changes in your plants. This can help shift your attention away from stressors.

- **Physical Activity:** Gardening involves various physical activities such as digging, planting, weeding, and watering. These activities provide gentle exercise that can boost mood and alleviate stress.

- **Sense of Accomplishment:** Seeing your plants thrive and your garden flourish can provide a sense of achievement and satisfaction, boosting your self-esteem and confidence.

- **Creative Expression:** Gardening allows you to express your creativity through design, choosing plants, and arranging garden elements in visually appealing ways.

- **Stress Reduction:** Research suggests that interacting with plants and being in green spaces can lower cortisol levels, the stress hormone, leading to relaxation.

- **Learning and Curiosity:** Gardening can be a continuous learning experience. Exploring different plants, understanding their needs, and experimenting with different gardening techniques can keep your mind engaged and curious.
- **Aesthetic Pleasure:** A well-maintained garden provides aesthetic beauty and a peaceful environment that can uplift your mood and create a tranquil sanctuary.
- **Therapeutic Solitude:** Gardening can provide a peaceful escape from the demands of daily life. Spending time alone with your plants can be a form of self-care and relaxation.
- **Problem-Solving Skills:** Overcoming gardening challenges, such as dealing with pests, choosing appropriate plants for your climate, and troubleshooting growth issues, can enhance your problem-solving skills.
- **Sense of Community:** Joining gardening clubs, participating in community gardens, or sharing gardening experiences with friends and family can foster a sense of belonging and connection.
- **Seasonal Rhythms:** Gardening allows you to connect with the natural cycles of the seasons, which can help you feel more grounded and in tune with the world around you.
- **Positive Distraction:** Immersing yourself in gardening tasks can redirect your focus away from stressors, providing a positive distraction and a break from worries.
- **Harvest and Rewards:** If you're growing edible plants, the act of harvesting and enjoying the fruits of your labour can be highly rewarding and satisfying.
- **Environmental Contribution:** Gardening contributes positively to the environment by supporting pollinators,

reducing carbon emissions, and promoting biodiversity.

Whether you have a small balcony garden, a backyard plot, or just a few potted plants indoors, the act of nurturing and caring for plants can have a significant impact on your well-being. The process of watching life grow and change can mirror your own journey and provide a sense of tranquillity and renewal.

Spirituality and devotional practices

For many people, engaging in a devotional practice centred around their faith and spirituality can provide a sense of comfort, guidance, and stress relief. Here are some ideas for incorporating a devotional practice into your life for stress relief, specifically focused on a God-centred approach:

- **Daily Prayer:** Set aside time each day for prayer. This can involve expressing gratitude, seeking guidance, and offering your concerns and worries to God.

- **Meditation:** Practice meditation with a focus on God or a particular scripture. Use calming phrases or verses to quiet your mind and connect with your spiritual beliefs.

- **Scripture Reading:** Spend time reading sacred texts from your faith tradition. Reflect on the teachings, stories, and wisdom they offer. Choose passages that bring you comfort.

- **Journaling:** Keep a journal to write down your thoughts, prayers, and reflections. This can be a way to process your feelings and seek insights from a higher power.

- **Chanting or Singing:** Incorporate chants, hymns, or spiritual songs into your routine. The rhythm and melody can have a soothing and uplifting effect.

- **Mindful Worship:** Attend religious services or gatherings to engage in communal worship and connect with others who share your faith.

- **Acts of Kindness:** Engage in acts of kindness and service as a way to embody your faith and alleviate stress through selflessness.

- **Nature Walks:** Spend time in nature and see the beauty of creation as an expression of God's presence. Use this time for reflection and gratitude.
- **Guided Devotion:** Use devotionals or spiritual literature that provides daily readings, reflections, and prayers aligned with your faith.
- **Breath Prayer:** Create a simple prayer that you can repeat in sync with your breath. For example, inhale "God's peace" and exhale "fills me."
- **Candle Meditation:** Light a candle and focus on its flame as a symbol of divine presence. Let your worries melt away as you gaze at the flickering light.
- **Prayer Beads or Rosary:** Use prayer beads or a rosary to guide your prayers and keep you centred on your devotion.
- **Gratitude Practice:** Start or end your day by listing things you're grateful for. Acknowledging blessings can help shift your focus away from stress.
- **Quiet Retreat:** Set aside time for a quiet retreat or spiritual retreat where you can immerse yourself in prayer, reflection, and connection with God.
- **Visualization:** Close your eyes and visualize God's presence and protection surrounding you. Imagine yourself releasing stress and receiving divine peace.

Remember that your devotional practice should feel meaningful and authentic to you. It's about nurturing your spiritual connection and finding solace in your faith. Adapt these suggestions to align with your beliefs and traditions, and create a routine that supports your well-being and helps alleviate stress.

Debt free life

Achieving a debt-free life can indeed significantly reduce financial stress and contribute to overall well-being. Debt can be a major source of anxiety and worry, and working towards becoming debt-free can provide a sense of freedom and financial security. Here are steps you can take to work towards a debt-free life and experience stress relief:

- **Assess Your Debts:** Make a list of all your debts, including credit card balances, loans, and other liabilities. Note the interest rates and minimum payments for each.

- **Create a Budget:** Develop a comprehensive budget that outlines your monthly income, expenses, and debt payments. This will help you understand where your money is going and identify areas for potential savings.

- **Prioritize Debt:** Determine a debt repayment strategy. You can use methods like the debt snowball (paying off the smallest debts first) or the debt avalanche (paying off debts with the highest interest rates first).

- **Cut Unnecessary Expenses:** Look for ways to reduce discretionary spending and allocate those savings towards debt repayment. This might include dining out less, cancelling unused subscriptions, or finding more cost-effective alternatives.

- **Increase Income:** Explore opportunities to boost your income, such as taking on a part-time job, freelancing, or selling items you no longer need.

- **Negotiate Interest Rates:** Contact creditors to negotiate lower interest rates on your debts. This can help reduce the overall cost of repaying your debts.
- **Build an Emergency Fund:** While focusing on debt repayment, also work towards building an emergency fund. Having savings for unexpected expenses can prevent you from relying on credit cards or loans during emergencies.
- **Consolidate or Refinance:** Explore options for consolidating multiple debts into a single loan with a lower interest rate. Refinancing can help save money on interest payments.
- **Stay Committed:** Stick to your debt repayment plan even when it feels challenging. Consistency is key to making progress and eventually becoming debt-free.
- **Celebrate Milestones:** Celebrate each debt paid off as a significant achievement. This positive reinforcement can help you stay motivated.
- **Avoid New Debt:** While paying off existing debt, avoid taking on new debt unless absolutely necessary. This prevents the cycle of debt from continuing.
- **Seek Financial Advice:** If your debt situation is complex, consider seeking advice from a financial advisor or credit counsellor. They can provide personalized guidance based on your circumstances.
- **Stay Patient:** Becoming debt-free is a journey that takes time. Be patient and remember that every step you take is bringing you closer to your goal.
- **Practice Self-Care:** Engage in stress-relieving activities that don't involve spending money, such as meditation, spending time with loved ones, exercising, or enjoying hobbies.
- **Celebrate Your Debt-Free Life:** Once you've paid off your

debts, celebrate your accomplishment. Reflect on the stress relief and newfound financial freedom you've gained.

Becoming debt-free requires commitment, discipline, and a willingness to make changes in your financial habits. It's a process that takes time, but the relief and peace of mind that come with achieving a debt-free life are well worth the effort.

Financial planning

Financial planning plays a crucial role in reducing stress related to money matters. When you have a clear financial plan in place, you can make informed decisions, manage your finances more effectively, and alleviate worries about your financial future. Here are steps you can take for effective financial planning to experience stress relief:

- **Set Clear Goals:** Define your short-term and long-term financial goals. This could include saving for emergencies, retirement, education, a home, or a vacation.
- **Create a Budget:** Develop a budget that outlines your monthly income and expenses. This helps you track where your money is going and identify areas for potential savings.
- **Build an Emergency Fund:** Save three to six months' worth of living expenses in an easily accessible account. An emergency fund provides a safety net during unexpected situations.
- **Manage Debt:** Create a plan to pay off high-interest debt. Prioritize paying down credit card balances and loans to reduce interest payments over time.
- **Save for Retirement:** Contribute regularly to retirement accounts, such as a 401(k) or an Individual Retirement Account (IRA). Starting early can lead to a more secure retirement.
- **Invest Wisely:** If you're comfortable with investing, develop an investment strategy that aligns with your goals and risk

tolerance. Diversification can help manage risk.

- **Automate Savings:** Set up automatic transfers to your savings and investment accounts. This ensures you consistently save and invest without having to remember each month.

- **Review and Adjust:** Regularly review your financial plan to track your progress and make necessary adjustments. Life circumstances change, and your plan should adapt accordingly.

- **Educate Yourself:** Continuously educate yourself about personal finance. The more you understand, the better equipped you'll be to make informed decisions.

- **Insurance Coverage:** Ensure you have adequate health, life, disability, and property insurance coverage to protect yourself and your family.

- **Estate Planning:** Create a will, designate beneficiaries, and establish powers of attorney to ensure your wishes are respected in case of incapacity or passing.

- **Manage Tax Implications:** Be aware of the tax implications of your financial decisions. Strategic tax planning can help you minimize your tax burden.

- **Stay Organized:** Keep important financial documents organized, including bank statements, tax returns, investment records, and insurance policies.

- **Limit Impulse Spending:** Practice mindful spending by avoiding impulsive purchases and evaluating whether an item aligns with your priorities and budget.

- **Seek Professional Advice:** If you're unsure about financial matters, consider seeking advice from a financial advisor who can provide personalized guidance.

- **Practice Self-Care:** Engage in stress-relieving activities that don't involve spending money. Engaging in hobbies, exercising, or spending quality time with loved ones can help manage stress.

- **Stay Positive:** Maintaining a positive mindset about your financial journey can help reduce stress. Focus on your progress and celebrate your achievements.
- **Practice Patience:** Financial planning is a long-term endeavour. Be patient and recognize that achieving financial stability takes time.

By taking control of your financial situation through thoughtful planning and informed decision-making, you can minimize financial stress and enjoy greater peace of mind. Remember that everyone's financial journey is unique, so tailor your plan to your individual goals and circumstances.

Strategy for inner peace

Attaining inner peace is a lifelong journey that involves cultivating a sense of calm, balance, and contentment within yourself. Here are some strategies that can help you foster inner peace:

- **Mindfulness and Meditation:** Practice mindfulness meditation to be fully present in the moment without judgment. Regular meditation can help calm your mind, reduce stress, and enhance self-awareness.
- **Self-Acceptance:** Embrace yourself as you are, including your strengths and imperfections. Self-acceptance promotes a positive self-image and reduces inner conflict.
- **Letting Go:** Learn to release attachment to outcomes, resentments, and things beyond your control. This can free you from unnecessary emotional burdens.
- **Gratitude:** Focus on what you have rather than what you lack. Regularly acknowledging the positive aspects of your life fosters contentment.
- **Simplify Your Life:** Declutter your physical space and your schedule. A simplified lifestyle can help reduce stress and create space for inner peace.
- **Healthy Boundaries:** Set and maintain healthy boundaries to protect your well-being. Saying "no" when necessary and valuing your own needs are important aspects of inner peace.
- **Positive Relationships:** Surround yourself with supportive and positive individuals who uplift you. Nurture

relationships that bring joy and connection.

- **Nature and Quiet Time:** Spend time in nature and engage in activities that allow you to experience silence and solitude. Nature has a calming effect on the mind.
- **Mindful Breathing:** Practice deep, conscious breathing to calm your nervous system and bring your attention back to the present moment.
- **Forgiveness:** Let go of grudges and forgive yourself and others. Forgiveness promotes emotional healing and reduces emotional weight.
- **Physical Well-Being:** Prioritize regular exercise, balanced nutrition, and sufficient sleep. A healthy body can contribute to a calm and clear mind.
- **Creative Expression:** Engage in creative activities that bring you joy, whether it's painting, writing, playing music, or gardening.
- **Compassion:** Extend kindness and compassion to yourself and others. Practicing empathy and understanding fosters connection and reduces conflict.
- **Limit Media Consumption:** Be mindful of the media you consume. Excessive exposure to negative news can impact your mental state.
- **Practice Patience:** Cultivate patience with yourself, others, and the circumstances of life. Patience reduces stress and anxiety.
- **Focus on What You Can Control:** Direct your energy toward things you can influence, and let go of things beyond your control.
- **Learn and Grow:** Continuously seek personal growth through learning, self-reflection, and setting meaningful goals.
- **Disconnect Regularly:** Take breaks from technology to

create space for introspection and mindfulness.

Remember that inner peace is not about avoiding challenges or negative emotions; rather, it's about developing the tools to navigate them with greater ease. These strategies can guide you toward a more peaceful and centred way of living, but the journey itself is unique to each individual. Be patient with yourself and embrace the process of self-discovery and growth.

Art of happiness

The central theme of "The Art of Happiness" revolves around the idea that happiness is not solely dependent on external circumstances, but it can be cultivated through inner transformation and a shift in one's mindset. The book emphasizes the following key concepts:

- **Inner Peace and Compassion:** The Dalai Lama emphasizes the importance of cultivating inner peace and compassion as foundations for happiness. By cultivating qualities like empathy and kindness, individuals can create a positive environment for their own well-being and the well-being of others.
- **Understanding Emotions:** The book encourages readers to understand and manage their emotions rather than being controlled by them. Developing emotional intelligence allows individuals to respond to challenges with resilience and balance.
- **Mindfulness and Presence:** Mindfulness, the practice of being fully present in the moment, is highlighted as a way to reduce stress and anxiety. By focusing on the present, individuals can free themselves from past regrets and future worries.
- **Materialism and Satisfaction:** The Dalai Lama suggests that the pursuit of material wealth alone does not lead to lasting happiness. True satisfaction comes from cultivating positive

inner qualities and appreciating the simple joys of life.

- **Altruism and Connection:** Engaging in acts of kindness and forming genuine connections with others can contribute to a sense of purpose and happiness. Acts of giving and altruism lead to a sense of interconnectedness with all living beings.

- **Acceptance of Impermanence:** The book discusses the Buddhist concept of impermanence — the understanding that everything in life is transient. Embracing this concept can help individuals let go of attachment and reduce suffering caused by expectations.

- **Overcoming Negative Emotions:** The book provides insights on managing negative emotions like anger, jealousy, and resentment. Developing a sense of perspective and understanding the underlying causes of these emotions can lead to their transformation.

- **Gratitude and Contentment:** Practicing gratitude for the positive aspects of life and cultivating contentment with what one has contribute to a sense of well-being.

Overall, "The Art of Happiness" offers a blend of spiritual wisdom and psychological principles, presenting a holistic approach to finding happiness and contentment. The book suggests that happiness is not a constant state but rather a skill that can be developed over time through self-awareness, mindfulness, and compassionate actions.

Gratitude is the king

Indeed, gratitude is often considered a powerful and transformative attitude that can greatly influence our well-being and outlook on life. The concept of gratitude involves recognizing and appreciating the positive aspects of our lives, both big and small, and acknowledging the blessings and experiences we have.

Here are a few reasons why gratitude is often referred to as "the king":

- **Positive Perspective:** Practicing gratitude helps shift our focus from what we lack to what we have. This positive perspective can lead to greater contentment and a more optimistic outlook on life.
- **Stress Reduction:** Gratitude has been shown to reduce stress and anxiety. When we focus on the things, we are grateful for, it can help us manage our worries and promote a sense of calm.
- **Improved Relationships:** Expressing gratitude toward others strengthens our connections and relationships. It shows appreciation and fosters a sense of mutual respect.
- **Enhanced Well-Being:** Grateful individuals often report higher levels of overall well-being, including increased life satisfaction and happiness.
- **Resilience:** Gratitude can enhance our ability to cope with challenges and setbacks. It encourages a mindset that focuses on the positives, even in difficult situations.

- **Mindfulness:** Practicing gratitude encourages us to be present and mindful of the current moment. It helps us appreciate the little things that often go unnoticed.
- **Generosity:** Gratitude can inspire acts of kindness and generosity. When we recognize the good in our lives, we may feel compelled to give back to others.
- **Physical Health:** Studies have suggested that gratitude may have positive effects on physical health, including better sleep, reduced blood pressure, and a stronger immune system.
- **Emotional Regulation:** Gratitude can help regulate emotions, making it easier to manage negative feelings and cultivate a more balanced emotional state.
- **Cultivation of Happiness:** Gratitude is often associated with increased feelings of happiness. By appreciating what we have, we can experience a greater sense of joy and fulfilment.
- **Simple Practice:** Practicing gratitude doesn't require elaborate rituals. It can be as simple as keeping a gratitude journal or taking a moment each day to reflect on what you're thankful for.
- **Cultural and Spiritual Significance:** Gratitude is a central theme in many cultural and spiritual traditions around the world. It's often seen as a virtue that leads to a more meaningful and purposeful life.

By incorporating gratitude into your daily life, you can experience these benefits and more. It's a practice that can be cultivated through conscious effort and mindfulness, and it has the potential to bring about profound positive changes in your mindset and overall well-being.

About the Author

Atul Raghunathrao Waghmare is not only a seasoned professional but also a distinguished author in the fields of project management, software testing, and quality management. With a solid educational background, including a Master's degree in Computer Science, Atul has consistently demonstrated his expertise across various domains, including commercial and life insurance, banking, fintech, and more.